Biblical HR

"Brett Billups has masterfully created a blend of practical advice, biblical development, and encouragement. *Biblical HR* is a tremendous resource for Christians in the workplace, regardless of their role, level, responsibility, or specific workplace situation. Brett will help you see otherwise secular workplace challenges through the practical and invaluable lens of God's Word."

Shawn Hearn / *Former Chief Human Resources Officer – Michael's Stores, Inc., Founder G2G Consulting*

"Great advice, solutions, and pragmatic insights about how to lead as a Christ follower in the marketplace! In *Biblical HR*, Brett Billups has done the hard work of showing us how to let the Bible instruct us on our work life, and how to think about everyday issues. An invaluable resource for navigating the high-stakes concerns we face today in HR."

Telvin Jeffries / *Former Chief Human Resources Officer – Kohl's Corporation, Former Global Chief Human Resources Officer – RadioShack Corporation*

"Brett gives us a rich, biblical perspective of work, with excellent practical takeaways found at the end of each chapter. This book is a wonderful field guide that addresses many situations you may encounter in the workplace. His years of experience, humility, and thoughtful references from God's Word make *Biblical HR* a book worth keeping on your desk. You will pick it up often as you desire to make wise, gracious decisions as a Christian in the workplace."

Brad Payne / *President – College Golf Fellowship, Dallas Theological Seminary Board Member*

"*Biblical HR* is the book that managers (HR or otherwise) have been waiting for! While books on leadership abound with 20,000-foot-level platitudes, Brett Billups offers compelling guidance for tackling the most challenging issues in the workplace. His wisdom, grounded in biblical truths, serves as a definitive 'how to' and 'how to be' manual for leaders everywhere."

Dennis J. Trittin / *President – LifeSmart Publishing, Author* – What I Wish I Knew at 18: Life Lessons for the Road Ahead

"Brett's personality, gifts, and experiences uniquely equip him to write this book. Brett is able to take complicated issues and simplify them into simple action steps. I have greatly appreciated Brett's wisdom and counsel for many years. In *Biblical HR,* Brett uses relevant personal accounts that really help both explain and apply the principles in this book. Each of the principles in *Biblical HR* is based on Scripture and provides biblical authority. I recommend *Biblical HR* to anyone in leadership, especially those who oversee a team of people."

Glyn Knight / *Pastor of Congregational Care – Summit Point Church*

"*Biblical HR* is a gift to the business world. Billups shows pure courage for reminding Christians everywhere that the REAL answers to business challenges are right there in the Bible. He excellently organizes biblical truths to the everyday struggles in business, making easy connections for the reader. *Biblical HR* is a must read for the Christian leader."

Joe Kiedinger / *CEO – Prophit Company (Leadership Coaching), Inventor – Dignify, Author –* Brander in Chief *and* The Dignity Based Franchise

Putting the "human" back into human resources requires a biblical approach; think of *Biblical HR* as putting the soul back into how we should be treating people as HR leaders and companies as a whole. In Christianity, we hear the term 'Christlike' all the time, but we rarely use that thought process and translate it into the workplace. *Biblical HR is* a must read for you and your teams, long overdue!"

Jess Terry / *CEO and Principal – Blue Ocean Edge, EVP Operations - Rheia, Former Chief Human Resources Officer – Roundy's Supermarkets Inc., Former Chief People Officer – Taylor Morrison*

"Wow—as a former corporate HR professional, business leader, and small business owner, I can only wish that I had *Biblical HR* as a resource much earlier in my career. I am so grateful for this masterfully written work by my dear friend and brother, Brett Billups. As a man of conviction who lives out his faith, Brett not only provides us with sound biblical truth, the practical insights for application that he offers as a seasoned HR practitioner are priceless. In the age of an increasingly complex world of work, the truths in this book are so timely, and yet the principles here within are so timeless. Irrespective of your employment status, whether you are in a position of leadership and authority in your workplace or not—or even employed at all—*Biblical HR* is for you!"

Keith Daniels / *Former HR Executive, Small Business Owner, Directional Pastor, Member and Secretary of the Board of Trustees – The Southern Baptist Theological Seminary, Louisville, KY*

Biblical HR

APPLYING ETERNAL TRUTHS TO EVERYDAY WORK

Brett Billups

NASHVILLE

NEW YORK • LONDON • MELBOURNE • VANCOUVER

Biblical HR

Applying Eternal Truths to Everyday Work

Published in New York, New York, by Morgan James Publishing. Morgan James is a trademark of Morgan James, LLC. www.MorganJamesPublishing.com

www.BiblicalHR.com

Proudly distributed by Ingram Publisher Services.

Morgan James BOGO™

A **FREE** ebook edition is available for you or a friend with the purchase of this print book.

CLEARLY SIGN YOUR NAME ABOVE

Instructions to claim your free ebook edition:
1. Visit MorganJamesBOGO.com
2. Sign your name CLEARLY in the space above
3. Complete the form and submit a photo of this entire page
4. You or your friend can download the ebook to your preferred device

ISBN 9781631956829 paperback
ISBN 9781631956836 ebook
Library of Congress Control Number: 2021941218

Cover and Interior Design by:
Chris Treccani
www.3dogcreative.net

Editorial by:
Inspira Literary Solutions
Gig Harbor, WA

Cover Logo by:
Madison Biebel-Sylvester

Morgan James PUBLISHING

Builds

with...

Habitat for Humanity®
Peninsula and
Greater Williamsburg

Morgan James is a proud partner of Habitat for Humanity Peninsula and Greater Williamsburg. Partners in building since 2006.

Get involved today! Visit MorganJamesPublishing.com/giving-back

*Dedicated to all my brothers and sisters in Christ
who are seeking to honor and glorify God
in every aspect of daily life.*

Table of Contents

Acknowledgments

This project would not exist without the assistance and encouragement of a number of special people.

To my Pinnacle Forum brothers, thank you for the support over the years. Special thanks to Cole Campbell, Denny Hanrahan, and Stephen Casey for the feedback and encouragement to step out in faith. (Thanks for the book title, Stephen!)

Thanks to my dear friends, Mark Shorman, Bill Maselunas, and Mark Waller. Your edits and encouragement made the final product better. Tara Gallagher, thank you for your kind words from a Christian HR perspective. It was an extra push to the finish line.

Arlyn Lawrence, Tim Lawrence, the team at Inspira Literary Solutions, and Dennis Trittin, thank you all for the encouragement and advice to a first-time author. *Biblical HR* would never have gone this far without your support.

Shawn Hearn and Telvin Jeffries, you have become such dear friends and brothers in Christ. Your encouragement, counsel, and support pushed me beyond my comfort zone into a place that I could witness God's hand at work. This book would not be in print without you.

Special thanks to my son, Truett Billups, and my dear friend, Brian Honett. The two of you have been with me from the very beginning. My gratitude for your patience, encouragement, edits, and biblical counsel is beyond words. I look forward to many fruitful years with you in this endeavor.

Krissi, you are the love of my life, my best friend, and my loudest cheerleader. You believe in me when I don't. You have stood by me in good times and in tough times. Every year with you is a blessing from God. I can only look in wonder at the beautiful heart you have for Jesus and your love for others. You have my love and gratitude from the deepest parts of my heart.

If anyone gleans anything helpful from the contents of this book, it is only through the wisdom and guidance of my Lord and Savior, Jesus Christ. The precepts in this book are His wisdom, not mine. At times, I find myself having to read the contents of this book for my own edification, a testimony to His eternal Word. My sincere prayer is that this book increases your love for Him and His Scriptures and encourages the application of His Word to your daily life.

Introduction

"I don't know what to do. I really need help."

These were the words of a newly promoted manager I supported in my HR role. One of her employees had been accused of stealing product from a retail store that they serviced. The accusers claimed to have video evidence, but this long-term employee had never been accused of this before. The manager was new to a management role and was in a panic about how to handle the situation.

I have heard these words often in reference to HR employee relations situations in the workplace. In my experience, every employee situation is different—different personalities, different circumstances, and different dynamics. Each situation has the potential for unpredictable outcomes. In the case above, the evidence was too overwhelming, and the customer's position was unwavering to the point that we had to terminate a long-term and experienced employee. This was an unexpected blow to the manager and her team. However, this type of situation could happen at any time during the course of day-to-day work.

Dealing with workplace human resources issues is more like a game of chess than checkers. Every scenario has multiple players with varying moves. It is impossible to predict an individual's next move or reaction. In chess, individuals can achieve the title of Grandmaster through years of experience. But we will never master the ability to accurately evaluate and predict potential outcomes of human resources situations. We can become better, but no book, education, or class will make you a Grandmaster of people issues overnight.

The purpose of this book is to provide a biblical map, of sorts, for employees at every level to navigate common HR workplace issues. These principles could apply to your own personal employment and to your management of others. This is not step-by-step legal advice, only a guide. It is important to maintain communication with your human resources and legal departments with any HR related issue. My primary goal is that you are able to evaluate each situation with a godly mindset and maintain that attitude throughout the process, regardless of the trials or outcome.

Biblical HR started as a journey to find meaning and purpose in my own spiritual life versus secular work. I was becoming more and more disillusioned by the ultimate goal of secular work to operate strictly on a financial level with worldly goals. I wanted to escape from this type of temporal focus and strive for more eternal things. In my opinion, my cause was noble. I desired to apply my skills and abilities to pursue more "Kingdom-centered" ideals. I was weary of workplace politics, manipulation, weak leaders, and meaningless objectives that were not God-honoring. However, I could not find resources that encouraged me on a practical level.

There are many fine books and lectures on applying biblical leadership principles at a strategic and even organizational level. Many of these books or websites contain sincere biblically centered truth. But they come from a conceptual rather than practical perspective. I struggled to find a daily practical application of these concepts.

As I struggled, God taught me that applying biblical principles to my work *was* Kingdom-centered work. I could honor Him in how I counseled people to deal with specific workplace issues such as a difficult boss, a low-performing employee, how to hire the right person, or even letting someone go from the company. I decided to write on these subjects as a ministry to others who are struggling with their role in the workplace and to remind myself of God's sovereign faithfulness in my own life. I must confess, I find myself needing to read my own material from time to time to re-center my focus on this calling.

You are called to the same spiritual objective. You are called to further His Kingdom in the trenches of secular work. You are to be a light in a workplace that needs to know Christ. You are called to handle workplace situations through your relationship with Christ, not by worldly standards or corporate policies.

As a believer, you have a tremendous advantage over any corporate procedure and/or policy. We can lean on our relationship in Christ to help us discern the truth of a situation or issue through a godly lens. Don't underestimate the power of God's truth and the work of the Holy Spirit in dealing with workplace HR issues. Most believers in the workplace tend to rely *only* on workplace policies to dictate their actions in complex situations. It's much easier to follow an employee manual or written policy than work to discern the root truth of a situation. While it is necessary to consider and comply with organizational policies and procedures, the methods and actions to accomplish this compliance should be driven by our relationship with God. Rely first on the gift, wisdom, and discernment of the Spirit of God and His Word to guide you through any workplace issue.

We were created to use our God-ordained gifts for His glory in the workplace. We are to be firm examples of biblical principles in our employment. We are called to effectively lead an organization to long-term business health through the application of godly princi-

xviii | Biblical HR

ples. I pray that my experience encourages you to join in the original, created plan for work and embrace God's desire for His creation.

I realize that not every specific situation is addressed in this book. I did not tackle subjects such as substance abuse, love triangles, violence in the workplace, or conducting an investigation (among others). There are some extremely sensitive, complex, and volatile issues that most managers and employees are not equipped or experienced enough to address and should absolutely refrain from attempting to handle on their own. I have limited the subjects in this book to areas that managers and employees deal with on a regular basis and need basic guidance on handling. Most workplace issues fall into one of the articles included here. However, be prepared to communicate and escalate all workplace issues to your Human Resources and/or Legal Department. We can find ourselves outside of our jurisdiction very quickly and unexpectedly.

So, how do we practically apply the eternal gift of grace and mercy to the "thorns and thistles" of the workplace? How do we practically focus on biblical principles in dealing with specific issues like having a difficult boss or co-worker, being passed up for a raise or promotion, dealing with workplace rules and politics, a poor performance review (or even a good performance review), favoritism, and even political correctness? What about those things that are diametrically opposed to godly character and values? How do we become doers of the Word at work rather than hearers only at church?

Practically applying the gospel to workplace issues is something that everyone who works struggles with from time to time, myself included. The primary purpose of this book is to provide some biblical guidance and focus to honor God in the challenging world of work.

Chapter 1

A Biblical View of Work

The very mention of work stirs a range of emotions within us—everything from anxiety, fear, frustration, anger, pride, satisfaction, disappointment, discouragement, and a host of others. But God did not originally intend it to be this way. God is the author of work. He created it prior to the Fall for His purposes. It was not originally created to be a punishment or a consequence of sinful rebellion. Let us remind ourselves of His original desire for our work.

In the Garden of Eden, God created man to rule and have dominion over His new creation (Genesis 1:26). This was a great responsibility and honor. By introducing the concept of work, God invited us to participate in His creation by enjoying our God-given gifts to not only grow food to eat, but to grow His Kingdom. We are to encourage and build the Body of Christ, to sanctify His people, for the glory of God. Work was good! But after the Fall, because of our sin and rejection of God, our spiritual condition, and ultimately our work environment, changed dramatically. It became impossible for us to have the same working relationship with God. Genesis 3 tells us:

> *"Cursed is the ground because of you; in pain you shall eat of it all the days of your life; thorns and thistles it shall bring forth for you; and you shall eat the plants of the field. By the sweat of your face you shall eat bread, till you return to the ground, for out of it you were taken; for you are dust, and to dust you shall return."*
> *(Genesis 3:17b-19)*

We brought a tough life upon ourselves, which is more than a little discouraging. But Jesus Christ loved us enough to be born into a sinful world, to live and teach us His precepts, and to die on the cross as a penalty for our sins. He provided redemption from the rejection of Him that caused this environment and our spiritual condition. His desire is to regain the perfectly designed relationship He initially shared with us at creation. This redemption should be first and foremost in our minds and provide us a model for how we deal with any situation or issue, even in the workplace. The work of the cross has provided us with grace and mercy to last an eternity, and we are forever free from the burden of sin. The sacrifice of Christ is our only source of hope.

As he ends his book, *Knowing God*, J.I. Packer describes the only way that we can keep the priority of the gospel first and foremost in our minds.

> "Finally, we have been brought to the point where we both can and must get our life's priorities straight. From our current Christian publications, you might think that the most vital issue for any real or would-be Christian in the world today is church union, or social witness, or dialogue with other Christians and

their faiths, or refuting this or that ism, or developing a Christian philosophy and culture, or what have you. But our line of study makes the present-day concentration on these things look like a gigantic conspiracy of misdirection. Of course, it is not that; the issues themselves are real and must be dealt with in their place. But it is tragic that, in paying attention to them, so many in our day seem to have been distracted from what was, is, and always will be the true priority for every human being—that is, learning to know God in Christ."[1]

Our work life and the challenges it brings can easily fall into the category of a distraction. We run toward it or try to escape. It attracts us or repels us. It feeds our worldly desires or drains us spiritually. This turmoil tends to lead us away from God rather than to Him. We have forgotten His original, created desire for us.

According to the *Westminster Shorter Catechism*, "Man's chief end is to glorify God, and to enjoy Him forever."[2] This applies to our whole lives. It applies to our church life, our theology, our marriages, our parenting, our relationships, and even our work.

Work was originally intended to strengthen our relationship with our loving God and to enjoy Him forever. We have allowed the difficulty and complexity of secular work to distract us from this objective.

Our Biblical Response to Work

Before we can begin talking about specific workplace issues, it's important to remind ourselves of a few key biblical principles: God's sovereignty over all things, His gift of eternal salvation, and

---

1   Packer, J. I. *Knowing God.* InterVarsity, 1973, p. 279.
2   *Westminster Shorter Catechism*

the sanctification of His people. These basic principles can ground us to consider God's original intention of work.

In God's providence, He orchestrates and sustains every aspect of creation to glorify Himself. In this concept, He has ordained the job you have, the company you work for, and even the boss that has authority over you. How we respond to the workplace situations God has placed in our path reveals much about our heart attitude and belief in God's sovereignty. C.H. Spurgeon, in his sermon on Matthew 20:15, states:

> "There is no attribute more comforting to His children than that of God's Sovereignty. Under the most adverse circumstances, in the most severe trials, they believe that Sovereignty has ordained their afflictions, that Sovereignty overrules them, and that Sovereignty will sanctify them all." [3]

The sovereignty of God is a source of comfort in the face of trials or difficult workplace challenges. Learning to rest in His sovereign will for our lives is a lifelong lesson of trust and submission. By offering the eternal gift of salvation, Christ desires for every soul to spend eternity with Him. As Scripture reminds us:

> *"The Lord is not slow to fulfill his promise as some count slowness, but is patient toward you, not wishing that any should perish, but that all should reach repentance." (2 Peter 3:9)*

> *"This is good, and it is pleasing in the sight of God our Savior, who desires all people to be saved and to come to the knowledge of the truth."* *(1 Timothy 2:3-4)*

---

3   Spurgeon, C. H. *Divine Sovereignty*, "Sermon on Matthew 20:15."

So, remind yourself daily of the gracious gift of salvation you have been given and treat others as eternal souls precious to Christ. Boldly point others to Him with grace, mercy, forgiveness, and patience. Strive to consistently display this heart and attitude toward your co-workers, your boss, and your customers.

Through His supreme sovereignty and the gift of eternal salvation, God will use worldly circumstances and people to conform us to the image of Christ. This is part of Christ's sanctification plan for our lives:

> *"And I am sure of this, that he who began a good work in you will bring it to completion at the day of Jesus Christ." (Philippians 1:6)*

> *"And we know that for those who love God all things work together for good, for those who are called according to his purpose. For those whom he foreknew he also predestined to be conformed to the image of his Son, in order that he might be the firstborn among many brothers. And those whom he predestined he also called, and those whom he called he also justified, and those whom he justified he also glorified." (Romans 8:28-30)*

God has everything on earth at His disposal to mold us into the image of Christ, and loves us enough to use it all, even the most difficult workplace issues.

One important aspect to consider is that these principles are an application of the work of the Trinity in our lives. God has sovereignly designed the plan of salvation; Jesus Christ has performed the work; the Holy Spirit seals it. (We will not elaborate on this correlation here, but to study the work of the Trinity is definitely worthy of our time.) The Trinitarian work in our lives is important to consider lest we think that we have anything of value to contribute to the successful outcome of anything. The principles outlined in this book will not guarantee any resolutions; this work is best left to God alone. We must pray to that end. These suggestions are only a guide to set our hearts on Christ first and foremost as we walk through difficult HR issues.

SECTION 1

RELATIONSHIPS

Chapter 2

Being a Godly Leader

Countless books on leadership fill our shelves. They range from effective team leadership to the development of business strategy. There are books on how to lead non-profit businesses and volunteer organizations. There are a multitude of tests to determine your leadership style and development opportunities. Subject-matter experts range from successful leaders of large organizations to motivational speakers. The world offers many leadership programs that claim to ensure success. While the authors and speakers sell a lot of books and are awarded with many speaking engagements, the methods and results vary and are often ineffective long-term.

Most secular leaders and managers latch onto a method they believe works for them and their organization. They evangelize this process with passion, sometimes with impressive results, but again, not long-term. Soon, there will be a different leader with a different method with different objectives and results.

An effective leader is one who thinks and operates on a long-term strategy and develops short-term objectives to achieve that strategy. In a Christian sense, we are to think eternally but live temporally. Christ's objective is eternal. His desire is for all to be saved and have the gift of eternal life. But this requires humility and submission to God's glory.

How does this translate into godly leadership?

I have worked for senior leaders from a variety of back-grounds—those with both international and domestic experience, those who have worked in multiple organizations (public and private), family members who inherited the company, and those who have spent their entire leadership career in one organization.

Leadership can be broken down into one of two styles: a leader who thinks his way is the best, or a leader who realizes that his way might not be the best. The first group operates from a position of insecure pride, while the second understands that their position is one of humble servitude. The first leads teams from a hierarchical, directive approach while the second group intentionally fosters a collaborative environment.

Ineffective, Prideful Leadership

Prideful leaders are particularly good at protecting their own reputation. Some are good at short-term leadership roles with a variety of companies, while others grow their career within one organization.

Leaders who hop from one leadership job to another might be exceptional in achieving short-term results but cannot deliver long-term success. The reason that struggling companies hire external leaders or consultants to rebuild or turn around an orga-nization is that they were not effectively led in the past.

Leaders who have been promoted from within the company might understand the historical legacy of their organization, but legacy knowledge alone has limits when it comes to effectively leading a successful company. A good leader understands that leading an organization is more than applying historical or experiential knowledge. While there is value in learning from and not repeating mistakes, effective leadership is more than avoiding mistakes. A leader manages to what lies ahead, not always relating situations to what has historically occurred.

Pride is the enemy of godly, effective leadership. It inhibits good and well-meaning employees from contributing to an organization. It stifles productivity. It blinds leaders to efficient problem resolution. Prideful leaders immediately discount any idea that doesn't originate within the realm of their own experience, either out of ignorance, or fear of losing power and control.

Prideful, ineffective leaders are also hierarchical rather than collaborative. Based on their inability or failure to recognize necessary change, they dictate mandates in ways that maintain control. Prideful leaders have one style: subordinates are to follow orders. Insecure, prideful leaders believe that the only way to lead is to take command of a situation and tell others what to do. Subordinates are only there to fulfill their agenda. That type of style has its place in war or potentially life-threatening situations, but it unfortunately inhibits business growth.

I realize this may come across as a hyper-critical view of ineffective leaders. But in my experience, ineffective leadership directly impacts the health of an organization and the personal lives of all the employees. Effective leaders humbly recognize their faults and seek to "put to death" their pride for the sake of their organization and employees. I have seen too much organizational damage done and good employees lost under the guise of "leadership" to minimize its impact.

Godly Servant Leadership

The greatest leader who ever lived had something to say about leadership:

> *"You know that those who are considered rulers of the Gentiles lord it over them, and their great ones exercise authority over them. But it shall not be so among you. But whoever would be great among you must be your servant, and whoever would be first among you must be slave of all. For even the Son of Man came not to be served but to serve, and to give his life as a ransom for many." (Mark 10:35-45)*

This is a powerful passage on leadership. Christ directly contrasts worldly leadership to godly leadership. Worldly leaders expect people to serve them. You can witness this mentality in how they treat others. But Christ calls us to the exact opposite. His purpose was not to be served, but to serve. What does this really mean in a practical sense? Let's talk first about what servant leadership is not.

The worldly concept of servant leadership is a mischaracterization in many respects. It highlights a servant mentality toward our fellow man that at times may conflict with God's purposes. What some men want from their leaders is not always what is best. There are times when effective servant leaders must be strong in convictions against the odds. When Christ witnessed the moneychangers in the temple, He didn't offer to help them set up their tables or stage their inventory. He chased them out! He served the greater good, which was His Father, and not the desires of men. Servant leadership means serving God's objectives and not the objectives of men.

Sometimes a servant leader mentality manifests itself as a fear of men. A person might submit to the needs and desires of men in order to appease them and call it servanthood. This is simply an excuse to avoid confrontation and is a weak leadership position while claiming an attitude of humility. Servant leadership is serving God, not men—obeying God, not pleasing men. God calls us to serve others but only through His definitive lens. Not ours.

Take an inventory of your style. Are you an effective or ineffective leader? Do you display any of these characteristics? Have you asked those you trust for feedback? If you truly are one of these ineffective leaders, how truthful will your employees be with you? If your employees do not feel comfortable expressing their opinions or disagreements with you, that is a huge red flag. They do not believe that they will be heard—or worse, fear retaliation.

Conversely, if we are employed by an ineffective leader who displays some of these characteristics, how are we as believers to respond to him or her in a biblical way? We are to die to ourselves and serve them through Christ's example. We are called into a life of service to Christ. We are to die to our own agenda and expectations of others. (See Chapter 4: "Difficult Boss Relationship")

I will be the first to admit that this is difficult, especially to leaders who, in our opinion, are ineffective or prideful. We are called to honor God with our behavior and humbly submit to the leadership God has placed over us. Now, we are not called to be doormats or weakly submit to an abusive and ungodly leader who cares nothing about honoring God and encourages ungodly behavior. In his proposal to the commander of King Nebuchadnezzar's officials, Daniel was able to submit to an ungodly leader without compromising his faith (Daniel 1:8-21). Company loyalty is not blind loyalty, but rather transferred loyalty to Christ first and a worldly leader second. So, that's why a more accurate term than "effective leader" is becoming a "godly leader." Here are some examples of how godly leaders operate in the working environment.

1. Godly leaders foster a collaborative environment.

(Luke 10:21) A collaborative environment is one in which individuals are given clear direction on the mission by the leader. The leader then empowers and trusts these individuals to work toward accomplishing this mission. Opinions are openly discussed with no fear of ridicule or retaliation. Individuals are invested in each other to achieve a greater objective. They encourage, mentor, and support one another. This creates a powerful platform and culture. It dramatically strengthens their faith, love, and commitment to the leader's mission. Jesus provided this example masterfully in Matthew 10 when He sent out the disciples, and in Luke 10 when He sent out the seventy in pairs. Jesus Christ graciously allowed His disciples to participate in evangelizing the gospel of salvation. He gave them the mission of spreading the gospel message to specific people groups. He even provided the spiritual strength and authority to spread the gospel. He rejoiced in the Holy Spirit that things previously hidden were revealed.

2. Godly leaders humbly seek the best answer.

(Proverbs 5:12-14) Godly leaders want to hear different points of view and don't spurn correction or instruction. They may not accept or understand differing viewpoints, but they want to hear them out to ensure that they make the best decision possible with all of the information or data that they can gather. They also have a few trustworthy people that can provide sincere and honest feedback. They prayerfully consider this feedback and adjust if necessary.

3. Godly leaders seek continuous improvement.

(2 Peter 1:5-8) Godly leaders are always learning, and always growing, spiritually and professionally. This is the only path to continuous improvement, humbly recognizing that we all have much left to learn.

4. Godly leaders take the blame and responsibility for those in their charge.

(John 17:12) Christ took our penalty and judgment. Godly leaders assume responsibility for those that God has placed in their charge. Even though Christ bore no responsibility in our sin, He took the blame and bore it on the cross. Godly leaders stand in the gap for their employees.

5. Godly leaders show mercy.

(1 Corinthians 13:4-7) God showed mercy on us while we were yet sinners (see Romans 5:8). When well-meaning employees make a mistake in judgment or fail in an effort, godly leaders show mercy and grace in assuming that the individuals meant well and then correct appropriately. They don't immediately criticize and automatically condemn assuming that the individual was lazy or incompetent.

6. Godly leaders don't seek to glorify themselves.

(Philippians 2:3-8) Christ humbly submitted Himself as a sacrifice to God for our sins. This was for God's glory and our salvation, not for Himself. Godly leaders sometimes sacrifice themselves for the greater good of their employees or the company.

7. Godly leaders manage change.

(Acts 6:1-7) Change doesn't manage them. Times change, people change, methods change—everything changes. Consider whether the change is for the better or for the worse. Godly leaders anticipate and manage necessary productive changes to the organization or mission.

8. Godly leaders are disciplined, not reactionary.

(1 Peter 1:13-16, 4:7-10) Godly leaders don't emotionally react to their circumstances or allow their emotions to influence their actions. They prayerfully and patiently consider how to handle sensitive and complex situations, especially when it impacts their employees. Godly leaders prayerfully evaluate the current cultural and business environment and develop both long-term/short-term goals to meet organizational objectives. Measures and milestones are established and course corrections may be necessary if the business landscape changes. They don't pridefully maintain course hoping to prove that they were right. They don't forget they are a Christian when things get tough. There are leaders who claim to be Christians but when placed under stress, they revert to worldly methods to alleviate anxiety or control the desired outcomes.

9. Godly leaders are kind.

(1 Corinthians 13:4-7) "Kindness" is a word that is often associated with weakness. Strong, effective leaders are kind to others. When you witness a leader who is not kind to others that is a red flag. One CEO uses what he calls the "breakfast interview." He invites a job candidate to breakfast—but arrives at the restaurant early, pulls the manager aside, and says, "I want you to mess up the order of the person who's going to be joining me. It'll be okay, and I'll give a good tip, but mess up their order." His reasoning: "I

do that because I want to see how the person responds. That will help me understand how they deal with adversity. Are they upset, are they frustrated, or are they understanding? Life is like that, and business is like that. It's just another way to get a look inside their heart rather than their head."

10. Godly leaders weigh the cost and make godly decisions.

(Luke 14:25-33) Leaders still must make the final decisions and take responsibility for them. They cannot shirk that responsibility. Sometimes the decisions are easy, others are difficult. Sometimes there is a cost or sacrifice to making a godly decision. A wise, godly leader is willing and able to make that decision.

As Christians, we are to model the leadership of Christ. No better passage communicates the attitude of Christ's leadership than Philippians 2:3-8.

"Do nothing from selfish ambition or conceit, but in humility count others more significant than yourselves. Let each of you look not only to his own interests, but also to the interests of others. Have this mind among yourselves, which is yours in Christ Jesus, who, though he was in the form of God, did not count equality with God a thing to be grasped, but emptied himself, by taking the form of a servant, being born in the likeness of men. And being found in human form, he humbled himself by becoming obedient to the point of death, even death on a cross."

Godly leaders who are effective in the business world understand that while financial health is important, the goal is not how much money the business can make short term; it's honoring God in how you make it. Effective, godly leaders wisely understand that this is what leads to long-term business success and having an eternal impact. Godly leaders serve God first.

For Further Study

1. Read Philippians 3:1-8. What was Paul's reaction to his former worldly status of leadership?
2. Read 1 Samuel 16: 1-13. What is God seeking in a leader?
3. Read Daniel 1:1-21, 3:1-30, and 6:1-28. How did God honor Daniel and his friend's obedience? Were they certain of God's deliverance?
4. Read Hebrews 11. Describe the consequences of living by faith.
5. Read Matthew 10 and Luke 10. Describe the collaborative environment that Jesus created among His disciples.

Chapter 3

Dealing with Difficult Co-workers

I once dealt with a co-worker who, in my opinion, was harsh, intimidating, and belittling to her employees. In response, they reacted to her out of fear rather than loyalty. Since I was the Human Resources Manager for the facility and responsible for the employee culture, certain employees confided in me about how this behavior was negatively impacting the employees and the business. Changes needed to be made.

I made several appeals to her direct supervisor to have this manager replaced, but he adamantly told me that this was not going to happen. So, the supervisor and I attempted to coach her to manage people in a more positive way. She did what we asked her to do, but I did not have any confidence that she was taking this change to heart, and that she was only "going through the motions" to keep her job. Her opinion and treatment of me was very adversarial. She considered me a "soft" HR manager with employees, but conversely "out to get her fired." We eventually brought in an outside consultant to work one-on-one with her.

This helped somewhat, but it was not enough. Her employees still did not trust her.

Shortly after her time with the consultant ended, she came into my office to speak with me. She sat down, holding back tears, and trying to maintain composure. After a few moments, she looked at me and said, "I'm not as bad of a person as you think I am." Without another word, she left. This caught me completely off guard. I started to question myself: Had I misjudged her? Why did she feel the need to express that to me now? Was she in any way repentant for her behavior? After years of reflecting on this event, I realized that I was treating her as an enemy–against me and against what I considered the proper way to manage people. I had become judge and jury to her behavior. With enemies, the natural reaction is to overcome them and win the fight. But Christ tells us something different:

> *"You have heard that it was said, 'You shall love your neighbor and hate your enemy.' But I say to you, love your enemies and pray for those who persecute you, so that you may be sons of your Father who is in heaven. For he makes his sun rise on the evil and on the good, and sends rain on the just and on the unjust. For if you love those who love you, what reward do you have? Do not even the tax collectors do the same? And if you greet only your brothers, what more are you doing than others? Do not even the Gentiles do the same?" (Matthew 5:43-47)*

In His Sermon on the Mount, Christ calls believers to a higher standard than what was traditionally taught at the time, to a perfect standard. It was considered normal behavior to love your friends and hate your enemies. But Christ taught that hatred for our enemies was a place for bitterness, jealousy, strife, or resentment to take root. The true test of our Christian walk is not how we treat our brothers and sisters in Christ, but how we treat and react to those who are openly hostile to us.

Christ Himself displayed this love in Luke 23:34. As the Jewish leaders were reveling in their perceived victory and His crucifiers were casting lots for His garments, He asked His Father to "forgive them, for they do not know what they are doing."

The most important point to remember as we deal with difficult co-workers is that we ourselves were once enemies of God and our sinful nature is still at war with Him. For while we were still sinners, Christ died for us (Romans 5:8). He extends the loving hand of grace, love, and mercy to creatures that don't deserve it. All of us have fallen short of the glory of God (Romans 3:23). All of us. Who are we to determine which of us are deserving or worthy of God's grace when we ourselves are not?

You might deal with similar individuals and situations. Your difficult co-worker might be a perpetually unhappy person who has an overall negative attitude and wants to make it known to everyone. You might have co-workers who hold grudges against you. An individual might be constantly trying to undermine or discredit you in some way. It might be an ungodly work environment with off-color jokes or shots about your Christianity and your "holier than thou" way of life. You might be frustrated with someone whom you deem to be lazy or incompetent. Your difficult co-worker might even be a professing Christian! This is especially hard because they are expected to practice their faith. You might be there to provide a gentle and loving reminder, but then again, they might need the gospel and truly not realize it. Here are some suggested ways to handle difficult co-workers:

1. Are you at fault in any way?

Are there any behaviors that you need to apologize for? Pray and ask God to reveal this to you. Repent and change this behavior to Christ-like attitudes (Matthew 7:4-5).

2. Don't go running to your boss every time something happens with this co-worker.

Be willing to confront them directly, but with a loving and respectful attitude. Appropriately challenge disrespectful behavior or actions. Point out how their behavior is impacting others and how that eventually impacts them directly by using specific examples. Use the same principle of Matthew 18 in your approach and suggest godly behavior instead. How they respond is their responsibility. Confronting destructive behavior is a loving thing to do. Avoiding it is not. (Note: there are a few sensitive issues that are best left for a supervisor to handle. Be wise, but don't pass it off because of fear.)

3. Remember the virtues of love.

Remind yourself that love is patient, kind, and gracious. Read 1 Corinthians 13.

4. Be gracious.

Don't revel when you believe they finally "get what they deserve." Be gracious and minister to them. (Proverbs 25:21-22; Romans 12:20).

5. Don't intentionally avoid them.

Don't intentionally avoid the difficult co-worker by taking a different route to the break room or scheduling a different time for lunch. This is a fear of man and only leads to more of the same

(Proverbs 29:25). Be courteous and pleasant when you encounter them in the hallway, break room, or worksite. Be cooperative when assigned to a project with them.

6. Include them.

Sincerely ask them for their assistance, input, or opinion on work projects. They might be resentful that they are not more engaged with what is going on with the business. One place I worked had an employee who was a constant complainer and had even filed legal action on the organization at one time. He regularly threatened to do it again, but he was very experienced in our business operations. Management started including him on more and more projects and it's amazing how his attitude turned.

7. Don't engage in the behavior to avoid the issue or conflict.

If you are at lunch or break and something inappropriate occurs, resist the temptation to join in or awkwardly laugh. You have the freedom to graciously excuse yourself from the scene.

8. Forgive them and forgive them again.

Christ displays an unlimited amount of patience and forgiveness to us that we are to display to others (Matthew 18:22).

9. Get to know them.

Ask questions. Use this knowledge to find ways to serve them and pray for them. It's not about you. Sometimes, our reactions to these situations actually reveal that we make our struggles with co-workers more about ourselves than we realize.

10. Appreciate personality differences.

Often, we have difficult co-worker relationships because we consider them different or even opposite from us. They just "rub us" the wrong way. That's our problem. Learn to understand and appreciate their strengths and forgive any personality quirks you find annoying. Perhaps this person has strengths opposite from yours (and vice-versa) that each of you can leverage.

11. Become aware of where bad behavior crosses the line.

Sometimes it is very appropriate to challenge or report harassing or intimidating behavior. If you are a witness to, or the recipient of, blatant harassing or intimidating behavior, be courageous enough to report it. You don't want to work in that type of culture, so protect yourself and others from it as well. There are federal laws and workplace policies in place to protect you in certain types of cases. Don't try and report it anonymously, there will not be enough information to conduct an investigation. Don't tell your boss, "I don't want you to do anything." They have an obligation to take action in certain situations.

12. Focus on Christ.

Difficult co-workers provide an opportunity to grow in our relationship with, and dependence on, Christ. Remember their eternal souls. Christ has promised to come again and right every wrong and judge all souls for eternity. Our faith and trust are in this promise, not our own view of immediate justice based on our terms. They need the gospel. The trial of difficult co-workers is temporary; eternity is not (Matthew 10:28).

Loving your enemies is displayed in acts of servitude and dying to ourselves, not in a feeling or an attitude. You cannot do this on your own effort. Pray that God grants you the ability to display His love through you. Our natural reaction is the one I had with my co-worker above: to defeat our enemies. But Christ has already fought this battle, and won, with His sacrifice on the cross. We can only love our enemies because He first loved us (1 John 4:19).

As I reflect on the crying former co-worker sitting in my office, I realize now that I did not treat or react to her out of a heart of love. I had judged her actions, did not approve of them, and was quickly willing to remove her from the picture and deal with her from my own self-appointed and self-righteous "judgment seat" (James 4:12). I was not interested in pointing her to, or modeling, Christ. Now obviously this does not excuse destructive behavior and I may have made the same recommendation at the end of the day but dealing with it from a biblical perspective may have had an eternal impact on her. I missed this opportunity.

Finally, consider this: Are they really your enemy? (Ephesians 6:12) I submit to you that they are not. That is the message that Christ is conveying to us in His teaching. When we sin, we set ourselves up against God, not men. Commentator R.C.H. Lenski says,

> "I cannot love a low, mean criminal who robs me and threatens my life, at least in the sense of liking him. I cannot like a false, lying, slanderous fellow, who, perhaps has vilified me again and again; but I can by the grace of Jesus Christ love them all, see what is wrong with them, desire and work to do them only good, and most of all, to free them from their vicious ways."

We can only do this by pointing them to the gospel of Christ, the only one who has set us all free.

For Further Study

1. Read Matthew 25:31-46. How does this encourage you to keep an eternal focus and keep difficult co-workers in perspective?

2. Read Acts 7:54-60 about the stoning of Stephen. How is Stephen's reaction an act of loving your enemies?

3. Read Luke 23:33-34. How is this an example of loving one's enemies and why does Christ say this?

4. Read Ephesians 6:10-17. Who is our real enemy and what are our weapons?

5. Do you ever believe that a difficult or immoral person "deserves" eternal separation from God?

Chapter 4

Difficult Boss Relationship

I once worked for someone who, in my opinion, had no clue what he was doing. I considered him incompetent, aloof, and someone who expected others to pick up his slack. After all, he had inherited the company and not really earned it. He provided no strategic direction or guidance and led with self-centered objectives. I had no respect for him and freely expressed my opinion. I spoke disrespectfully behind his back and did not submit to his leadership. I would have qualified him as an "unreasonable" boss. I'm ashamed to admit that I did not respond to this situation in a biblical way and ended up leaving the organization.

There are many passages of Scripture dealing with work and masters (or bosses) but let's focus on just one for this topic. In the book of 1 Peter, the Apostle Peter encourages persecuted believers to "prepare your minds for action" and "set your hope completely on the grace to be brought to you at the revelation of Jesus Christ" (1 Peter 1:13). Peter then goes on to tell us how to do to be godly witnesses and examples despite extreme persecution. Although most of our workplaces do not qualify as places of extreme persecution, there are biblical principles we can learn from in these words. I encourage you to read the longer passage in context (1 Peter 2:12-21), including:

> *"Servants, be subject to your masters with all respect, not only to the good and gentle but also to the unjust" (1 Peter 2:18).*

One caveat: We must remember the context of this passage. Peter is writing to Christians who have experienced, and perhaps fled, extreme persecution and oppression. This passage is "not" directing Christians that the "only" biblical option is to remain in an extremely oppressive or abusive environment. We are never commanded to blindly submit to human leadership. The Bereans questioned and verified apostolic teaching and pursued spiritual righteousness (Acts 17:11). Peter is stating that this particular situation is the "best" option for them right now and gives direction on how to deal with and handle it from a biblical perspective. So, if the best option for you right now is to remain in your current situation, there are appropriate biblical ways to handle it.

Scripture is clear on our responsibility to submit and be respectful to those in authority over us, for God in His providence has ordained our particular circumstances. This passage commands us to be submissive by putting ourselves in a subservient position of obedience (or doing what we are directed to do) and doing so with a respectful heart and attitude. Here are some specific ways that you can biblically display submission and respect:

1. Pray for your boss.

Pray for your boss, whether he or she is a believer or not. If not, pray specifically for salvation. If your boss is a believer, then pray that God grants wisdom to lead in a godly and biblical way.

It's hard to be angry at someone when you begin to pray for them (Matthew 5:43-45; Luke 6:27-28; 1 Timothy 2:1-4).

2. Understand your boss's expectations.

Understand the expectations your boss has for you and make every effort to not only achieve them, but exceed them! If you need to meet with your boss to clarify your work objectives, then do so. Meet on a weekly, or bi-weekly, basis if necessary to determine if you are on track. Prioritize the requests your boss asks of you and plan to do excellent work (1 Corinthians 10:31; Ephesians 6:5-8; Colossians 3:23).

3. Guard your speech.

Don't speak ill of, or gossip about, your boss to anyone, whether co-workers, friends, or family (Proverbs 20:19; Romans 1:29; 2 Corinthians 12:20; 1 Timothy 5:13; 2 Timothy 3:1-3).

4. Don't complain.

Don't grumble and complain about your work assignment or position (Philippians 2:14).

5. Drop the expectations!

No matter how many times you get angry at things your boss does, or how much you desire your boss to do things differently, you can't change your boss's behavior or management style. Stop fighting a battle you are not designed or equipped to win. Only God can change hearts through submission to Him.

6. Be selfless.

Be the type of worker that is a joy to supervise. Be a blessing to your boss and be concerned for his or her interests (Philippians 2:3-4).

7. Be humble and respectful.

If it becomes necessary to confront your boss about a work issue, do it privately, respectfully, and with a humble heart. Provide facts, not hearsay. Your boss may not even be aware of the issue that is causing harm to you or others. Your respectful and humble approach may be exactly what is needed to increase this awareness in a gracious way. If your boss responds negatively, express thanks for the time and leave. Don't argue! (Proverbs 27:17; Matthew 18:15-20; Titus 2:9-10)

8. Never be confrontational to your boss in a public forum.

There may be times to respectfully challenge your boss in public, but never be confrontational. If you are berated or criticized in public, remember Christ did not respond by defending himself or proving he was right—and He had every right to do so (Mark 14:61; Romans 12:17; 1 Timothy 6:1-2; 1 Peter 2: 21-23).

9. If necessary, resign or seek another position.

In the end, if you determine that you cannot willfully submit to your boss's leadership, then you must prepare to resign from the organization or move to another position. If your boss is behaving contrary to legal or biblical mandates (or asking you to do so), or if you have hardened your heart and chosen not to submit, then this is the only godly and honorable thing to do. (It is important to note that there are other biblical reasons for leaving an organization. Those are not discussed here. I would recommend that you seek godly counsel before making the decision to leave an organization.)

To put this in a practical example, when your boss comes to you in the eleventh hour of a project or job and tells you that you are not doing it according to his earlier direction when you are certain that you understood him perfectly, don't respond with anger. Don't desperately make attempts to prove yourself right or "stand up for yourself." Responding in a submissive and respectful way looks completely different than our natural reaction. Ask for clarification and repeat back what you understand the expectations to be. Make every effort to not only fulfill them, but do over and above what's been asked (Proverbs 16:14).

Your boss may be used to "bullying" or "intimidation" to get things done. Don't react to this, it only makes things worse. If you respond with grace and patience, with submissive words and a respectful attitude, you may be the only model of grace and mercy that they ever see, a true expression of the gospel, and that's much more important that proving yourself right (Matthew 5:7).

We must also remember this: we will never respect or submit perfectly. It's not our nature. There is only one who could ever do that, and He is our advocate in spite of our failure (1 John 2:1-3). Christ was the perfect representation of respect and submission to authority, being obedient even to the point of death on the cross (Philippians 2:8). He was showing us that God's way is better than our own, and submission to God reveals the gospel (Matthew 26:39). As a result of Christ's perfect obedience and submission, we have the gift of eternal life. Through Christ's sacrifice alone, God pours out His grace, mercy, and steadfast love.

So why even make the effort to be obedient to this command? Why would we even put up with an unreasonable boss and unreasonable expectations, to willingly submit to and respect their authority? The major reason is explained above: to honor and worship Christ's submission to the Father and His sacrifice on our behalf. Another is this: sacrificial love was extended to them as well, the same love He had for us while we were yet sinners (Romans 5:8). Remember, we are also sinners in need of a Savior.

> *"Remind them to be submissive to rulers and authorities, to be obedient, to be ready for every good work, to speak evil of no one, to avoid quarreling, to be gentle, and to show perfect courtesy toward all people. For we ourselves were once foolish, disobedient, led astray, slaves to various passions and pleasures, passing our days in malice and envy, hated by others and hating one another. But when the goodness and loving kindness of God our Savior appeared, he saved us, not because of works done by us in righteousness, but according to his own mercy, by the washing of regeneration and renewal of the Holy Spirit, whom he poured out on us richly through Jesus Christ our Savior, so that being justified by his grace we might become heirs according to the hope of eternal life." (Titus 3: 1-7)*

Only through fixing our hope in Christ are we even able to have any desire to be obedient and respectful to those in authority over us. In doing so, we can respond biblically and with humility, for the rest of the 1 Peter passage states:

> *"Servants, be subject to your masters with all respect, not only to the good and gentle but also to the unjust. For this is a gracious thing, when, mindful of God, one endures sorrows while suffering unjustly. For what credit is it if, when you sin and are beaten for it,*

you endure? But if when you do good and suffer for it you endure, this is a gracious thing in the sight of God." (1 Peter 2:18-20)

Trust in Christ and prove yourself to be a trustworthy and honorable servant to your boss, an example of grace and mercy, even to unreasonable ones. For this finds favor with God.

For Further Study

1. Read 1 Peter 2:12-22. List the reasons why we are to be subject to every human institution.
2. How does submission to those in authority over us display God's sovereignty?
3. Is the teaching of submission to those in authority over us a call to be passive or inactive?
4. Read Matthew 26: 36-46. How does Christ's submission reveal the gospel? What actions did He take and what was He preparing Himself for?
5. If God in His sovereignty, places us in authority under what we would define as an "unreasonable boss," is He trying to punish us into submission? (Read James 1:2-3 and 1 Peter 1:6-7.)
6. Compare 1 Peter 2:12-22 and Romans 13:1-7. What did you observe?

Chapter 5

Conflict Resolution

During the night shift of one of our manufacturing plants, two volatile employees engaged in a verbal altercation that almost led to blows. The altercation escalated to the point where they were threatening each other physically. Fortunately, a supervisor was nearby and separated the two employees. They were both sent home pending further investigation.

The next morning, I began the investigation. In the process of interviewing the individuals, I was told there were no other witnesses to the event prior to the supervisor intervening. I had to rely on the statements of the two individuals directly involved. Each blamed the other and their interpretation of events directly contradicted one another. After interviewing each of them, I realized there was no way to ascertain the truth. I eventually gave them both a final written warning stating that if either of them were engaged in another altercation of this nature, they would be immediately terminated. A few months later, one of them was involved in a physical fight in the plant parking lot and was terminated.

Employee conflicts are some of the most frustrating and complex situations that organizations must deal with. Some conflicts are petty and seemingly insignificant while others are serious enough to lead to physical altercations.

Situations involving conflict, more than others, demand a heavy reliance on the Spirit of God for wisdom and discernment. No two conflicts are the same. The issues vary and the individuals involved have different perspectives and opinions. The truth is extremely difficult to determine. I strongly encourage you to step back and pray before you take any action toward the resolution of a conflict.

If you eventually decide it is necessary to tackle a conflict resolution, seek appropriate godly counsel and be patient. Most conflicts are not as urgent as the one described above. Don't get intimidated or rushed into a rashly executed resolution. Many individuals will push the resolution that benefits them. Evaluate the issue from all angles and consider all the implications of potential solutions.

While there is an argument that can be made to "nip issues in the bud" before they become larger issues, we must be discerning as to the substantive impact of the specific issue on the larger business. If we seek to resolve personal employee issues that have not escalated to having a substantive impact to business productivity, then it will be a waste of everyone's time and energy. However, if the parties fail to address or correct the conflict on their own and it escalates to the point of impacting productivity of the business, then it will need to be addressed immediately. You can certainly counsel individuals in this regard. Coach individuals to some type of resolution but inform those involved that if it remains unresolved and begins to impact business productivity, then it will become a significant issue and actions will be taken.

The most important lesson I have learned in my years of dealing with workplace conflict is that not every conflict will be resolved. That is an important lesson. If we expect to sit down and have everyone live in perfect harmony after a few meetings or sessions, we will be sorely disappointed.

I certainly have fallen into the trap of thinking I can solve every conflict. I pridefully thought, *Surely with my experience and knowledge we can come to some type of understanding and resolve this issue. After all, this was in everyone's best interests and therefore people desire to resolve conflict, don't they?* It was always a blow to my pride and ego when things did not turn out as I expected. I felt as if I had failed.

Gary Thomas, in his book *When to Walk Away*, addresses this issue very well:

> "There's a certain messianic complex in many of us that thinks if we were more intelligent or a little holier, if we fasted and prayed a bit more, then everyone we shared the truth with would agree with us and welcome God into their hearts.
>
> That didn't happen for the real Messiah, and it certainly won't happen for us. It's okay to walk away when people resist the truth. And it's okay to let them walk away.
>
> It took a while for Jesus' followers to get this. They often remained more enamored with the people's response than Jesus' truth. For example, when Jesus challenged the way the Pharisees put human tradition over the commands of God, the disciples "warned" Him, "Do you know that the Pharisees were offended when they heard this?" (Matthew 15:12)

Listen to Jesus' response: "Every plant that my heavenly Father has not planted will be pulled up by the roots. Leave them; they are blind guides." (Matthew 15:13-14)

Leave them. You don't always have to stay and argue with unreasonable people who are offended by the truth."[4]

It's important to recognize this principle when attempting to resolve a conflict. God must plant the humble desire in someone's heart to be at peace with others before the successful resolution of a conflict can occur. Our job as believers is to place ourselves in a state of humility before we walk into any attempt at conflict resolution, whether we are directly involved in a conflict with someone or attempting to mediate a resolution.

Don't get me wrong. Our hope as believers is that people humbly and prayerfully seek godly resolution to conflict. We are to desire reconciliation. We are to sincerely undertake efforts to pursue this peaceful resolution and keep it foremost in our hearts and actions. In fact, we are commanded to do everything we can to live at peace with all men. Failure to do so is a reflection on our relationship with God (Matthew 5:9; Hebrews 12:14; James 3:17). However, be prepared to recognize the lack of effort or desire of others to pursue the same, godly goal. If we prayerfully and faithfully attempt to resolve conflicts in a godly manner, we have not failed in our efforts if conflicts remain unresolved.

In my career, I have had to deal with employees stealing food from the refrigerator, employees not cleaning the microwave after heating their food, senior executives disagreeing on workplace pol-

---

4   Thomas, G. *When to Walk Away: Finding Freedom from Toxic People.* Zondervan, 2019, p. 20.

icies and the enforcement of them, and even love triangles gone awry. All workplace conflicts boil down to one common denominator: one individual or group attempting to push their desires or expectations onto another.

I have had many conversations with employees who have a conflict with a co-worker. Sometimes the issues are so trivial that I can't help but shake my head at the time and energy that have been wasted. We, as believers, are to handle conflicts differently than the way the world handles conflicts.

I will present this issue from two different perspectives because they are completely different in their methods of address:

1. Conflicts in which you are directly involved.
2. Conflicts you are attempting to resolve between two or more parties.

Let's first address conflicts in which you are directly involved. Paul challenges us:

"Repay no one evil for evil, but give thought to do what is honorable in the sight of all. If possible, so far as it depends on you, live peaceably with all. Beloved, never avenge yourselves, but leave it to the wrath of God, for it is written, 'Vengeance is mine, I will repay,' says the Lord. To the contrary, 'If your enemy is hungry, feed him; if he is thirsty, give him something to drink; for by so doing you will heap burning coals on his head.' Do not be overcome by evil, but overcome evil with good." (Romans 12:17-21)

Verse 18 is key: "If possible, so far as it depends on you, live peaceably with all." William Hendrickson says:

"There are circumstances under which the establishment or maintenance of peace is impossible. Hebrews 12:14 not only advocates peace but sanctification. The latter must not be sacrificed in order to maintain the former, for a peace without sanctification (or holiness) is not worthy of the name. If the maintenance of peace means the sacrifice of truth and/or honor, then peace must be abandoned (Matthew 10:34-46; Luke 12:51-53).

There are situations that require the sacrifice of peace. But we must be sure that it is not we who are to blame for such exigencies. We have done everything in our power to establish and maintain peace. The other person (or persons) was (were) not willing to have peace except on conditions we, as Christians, were unable to accept. In such cases God does not hold us accountable for the lack of peace." [5]

When we conflict with another person, even an unbeliever, our initial response should be to die to ourselves and our own desires and to seek within our own hearts for any fault, even if the other party has "done evil." We are not only to avoid any vengeful actions or speech toward others, but to do good to them! But not at a sacrifice to the truth of God. If we are faithful to this end, the result is left up to the One who judges justly (Romans 2:16, 3:26; James 4:12; 1 Peter 2:23). This is an accurate display of our attempt to have done everything humanly possible to resolve the issue.

Admittedly, our first human reaction is to stand up for ourselves and the wrongs done to us. There is a time and place to do

5   Hendricksen, W. *Romans New Testament Commentary*, Baker Academic, 1980, p. 421.

this in a humble and godly manner, but this is not our first or initial response. No one is perfect. Have you done anything, intentionally or accidently, to contribute to the conflict? (1 Thessalonians 4:6; Hebrews 10:30). Here are some practical steps to take:

1. Pray for God to reveal any fault that you should assume.

Through prayer and fasting, ask God to reveal your sins. Seek godly counsel for advice and perspective. Confess your sins to Him and repent of any further desire to commit them. There are situations where one party is entirely at fault. Pray especially in these situations that you have a godly response and reaction while remaining faithful to God's truth.

2. Ask for forgiveness.

Admit your wrongdoing and humbly ask the injured party for forgiveness. Even if they are not willing to extend forgiveness to you, confess, repent, and seek forgiveness regardless (Matthew 5:39).

3. Seek to restore.

If your actions have resulted in a loss to another individual, financially or otherwise, it is your responsibility to make restitution for this loss. Have you falsely implicated or accused others of wrongdoing? Correct the falsehoods. Have you gossiped or spoken ill of anyone in any regard that has caused harm? Repair the damage as far as you are able.

4. Be gracious.

You could very likely learn that this individual has a personal situation for which they need help or prayer. What a wonderful opportunity to share the gospel! If we are angry and adversarial in the face of conflict with another, we will most certainly miss an opportunity to extend grace and mercy to someone who truly needs it.

5. Keep the ultimate goal in mind.

Remain calm and humble. Christ knew His cause was right and just, but He kept the mission of the gospel at the forefront. There was no need to be angry or ask God to send a legion of angels to defend Him. His end goal was greater. He sought eternal salvation for all who believe (Matthew 26: 51-53, 27: 13-14; Mark 15:4-5).

6. Don't take on any responsibility that is not yours.

Just because you are a professing Christian and you are called to die to yourself and remain humble does not mean you automatically assume all the responsibility for the conflict. Sometimes in the face of conflict, the other person's first reaction is to protect themselves. This leads to a deflection of responsibility, and potentially, false accusations against you. Don't take this on. If you do, this compromises God's truth and does not lead to real peace (Ephesians 4:25-27).

7. Defend yourself appropriately.

Humbly state the true facts and your responsibility, but denounce any false accusations with supporting facts and data to the extent possible. Seek God's glory, not your own. Pray and seek God's justice regarding the conflict, not what is best for you or what protects you. God is a just judge. Rest in His hands.

8. Be willing to live with unresolved conflict.

If you have searched your heart and you have done everything within your power, the conflict still might not get resolved. This is okay. You have done your part. Move on. But moving on does not release us from the command to love our enemies. Continue to pray for the heart of your enemies and in doing so "heap burning coals" on their heads (Romans 12:20). If it is someone with whom you work closely, ensure that your manager realizes the steps you have taken to resolve the conflict. It is now out of your hands. Trust the final resolution to the One who judges righteously (1 Peter 2:23). Focus on your work and the work of the Kingdom.

Now let's discuss attempts to mediate conflict with others.

A former mentor of mine told me a story of a conflict he had with a co-worker. He and this co-worker had difficulty cooperating with one another in the work environment and disagreed on the implementation of company initiatives. Their animosity for one another was well known within the division. My friend was one of several senior level executives that reported to a National Divisional Leader in a well-known public organization.

This divisional leader decided to handle this conflict in a unique way. He scheduled a meeting with the two of them for 8:00 a.m. one Saturday morning in his office. As my friend and his co-worker entered the leader's office, they noticed a fresh, hot pot of coffee had been delivered and placed on the office conference table. Two cups were provided. He told them he wanted them to sit down and talk until their issues with one another were completely resolved. He told them that if the issues were not resolved by the time they left the table, then he would resolve the problem in his own way. The two of them sat in silence for a few moments, looked at each other, and told the leader that they got the message. He nodded and they left his office. The leader very effectively placed responsibility for the issue of conflict resolution in the laps of the parties involved.

When individuals come to you with a co-worker conflict, most of the time they are either hoping or expecting you to resolve it, or at least help them to resolve it. Don't automatically take that burden on. If resolution is in the best interest of the organization, or if the conflict is inhibiting productivity, then it may be necessary to intervene. However, don't let your pride step in and attempt to solve a problem that isn't yours to resolve. This only complicates things. People who want to avoid confrontation hope that others take on their problems and solve their issues for them.

It's important to remember that it is ultimately not your responsibility to resolve the conflict. It is the responsibility of the parties involved. These parties must come to realize that the issues center on their personal (even sinful) wants and desires. If the involved parties cannot admit to this fact, then successful and complete resolution/restoration is simply not possible. James talks about this very root cause.

> *"What causes quarrels and what causes fights among you? Is it not this, that your passions are at war within you? You desire and do not have, so you murder. You covet and cannot obtain, so you fight and quarrel. You do not have, because you do not ask. You ask and do not receive, because you ask wrongly, to spend it on your passions." (James 4:1-3)*

James rightly points out that the root cause of all conflicts is the sinful desires of our hearts to seek our own pleasures and desires. People fight and quarrel to get what they think they deserve. Some people are even willing to commit murder to appease these desires.

I am very often amazed at the fact that any workplace conflict is resolved at all. Most never truly are; they simply go underground.

As a believer, as I mediate a conflict or initiate an investigation, I rely on the discernment of the Holy Spirit within me to get some semblance of the truth. There is no way to completely ascertain the hearts and motives of others, however understanding that all conflicts reflect sinful desires of the heart is the right place to start. How unbelievers navigate these waters without the power of the Holy Spirit is beyond me. Here are principles for mediating workplace conflict:

1. Determine how significant it is.

You might be surprised to learn that, as we discussed, you do not have to resolve every workplace conflict. If it impacts the business and productivity, then it warrants involvement. If it could negatively impact a customer, then it will need to be addressed. Outside of that, I leave it to the individual parties to address.

2. Sometimes a simple reminder of the "Golden Rule" can de-escalate a situation.

This helps individuals shift their focus to others while applying the same moral principle to themselves that they expect of others. Simply ask the question, "Are you treating him or her the same way that you would expect to be treated?" Ask the employee to put themselves in the other individual's shoes.

3. Understand they may not have all the information.

One of the parties may be lacking some information or data. There might be some underlying personal reasons that have caused an individual to not meet another's expectations. Perhaps an individual or their immediate family member has a serious illness. Perhaps they just lost a loved one or are going through a messy divorce. Don't betray any confidences, but you can certainly remind others to consider their co-worker's personal situation without compromising any confidential information. Most people are willing to offer some grace after being reminded of this.

4. Coach others to resolve the conflict in a productive manner.

If the individuals cannot resolve the conflict on their own, inform them that if it eventually escalates to the point that you or their direct manager needs to get involved, then decisions could be made that negatively impact all parties.

5. Get the facts.

If you, Human Resources, or a manager must get involved, ask questions of the parties separately to get to the facts of the issue. If there is conflicting information, ask for the names of witnesses. Interview them as appropriate to gather more data. Schedule a meeting with all parties involved to listen, and clarify, each perspective.

6. Search for any underlying motives or objectives to the actual issue.

This is where it can get tricky. As James indicates above, the source of conflict is our sinful hearts and motives. You will need to ask some probing questions to drill down to the actual underlying issue.

- What is the actual conflict?
- What is the source of the conflict?
- Is there simply a misunderstanding?
- What is each party trying to accomplish?

- Why have you not been able to resolve this issue?
- How can this be accomplished another way?
- Is there a way to satisfy both parties? If not, what is the right decision for the business?
- Is this a higher-level directive that you disagree with?
- Is there a personal motive or incentive that benefits one side or the other?
- Is the long-term success of the business the primary objective?

7. Seek a solution.

After you get the facts or determine an underlying objective, seek a compromising solution. If that cannot be achieved, then the employee's manager or Human Resources may need to get involved (if they aren't already). A directive may need to be issued with formal disciplinary consequences for failure to comply.

8. Address the actions, not the motivation.

If individuals stubbornly refuse to resolve a conflict or fail to comply with the company's directive to work professionally and submit to cooperation with one another, then the motivation doesn't matter. Communicate the actions and/or behavior that is expected to occur and hold each party accountable to those expectations. This may lead to disciplinary action up to termination.

Remember, you cannot control the outcome of conflict resolution. You cannot expect to resolve every issue successfully. That is simply a prideful, naïve expectation and belief. It is ultimately the work of God in someone's heart that seeks to resolve conflict, not any man-centered wisdom or effort. Through our efforts, we can only determine if someone truly seeks resolution or not.

Be willing to walk away from any attempt to resolve the issue and deal with it based on the reality of the moment. Expect certain behaviors and/or actions in the meantime but continue to be available to coach the parties to a successful resolution if the opportunity presents itself.

Finally, don't make any decisions to intervene or take steps to resolve workplace conflict without seeking the counsel of God and the discernment of the Holy Spirit. Be sure that you seek His will for resolution and do not rely solely on experiential wisdom and corporate policies. Seek and honor God through every step of the conflict resolution process. He knows the best outcome to glorify Himself and further His Kingdom.

For Further Study

1. Read Galatians 2:11-21. What was Paul's issue with Peter and how did he handle it?
2. Read Matthew 18:15-17. What is the process for handling conflict between believers? How can this be applied in the workplace?
3. Read Mark 9: 33-37. How did Christ resolve this conflict?
4. Read James 2:12-16. How does this apply to an attempt to resolve conflict?

SECTION 2

EVALUATING

Chapter 6

Conducting a Performance Review

The employee was shocked. She did not understand why she had received a poor performance review when she sincerely believed she had tried so hard and had done so much to service the other employees. I tried my best to explain why I had given her a negative review, but to no avail. She remained terribly upset. Through tears, she kept saying that she did not understand.

I learned a valuable lesson that day. She was upset because I had blindsided her. I realized that I had not been giving her regular feedback. I relied on myself and others to fill the gaps in processes that she left undone, without confronting the poor performance. This left her completely surprised. I had also lost the opportunity to correct the issue long before the review. This would have saved a lot of wasted time and effort on my part and the other team members. I was not prepared or equipped to provide a productive performance review.

Without proper preparation, giving a performance review can be as nerve-racking as receiving one. Laying the groundwork beforehand is key. A good manager wants to provide encouraging feedback while pointing out areas where an employee can improve. A poor manager will use this time to berate or punish an employee.

The goal of all manager-employee interaction is to have a positive and productive employee for the organization. Your job as a manager is to give your employees that opportunity through regular feedback, coaching, and appropriate resources. It is then the employee's responsibility to respond and either continue a positive upward trajectory or make the necessary changes to achieve this goal.

As a manager, it is important that you understand the tremendous level of influence you have in this process. We cannot take this responsibility lightly. Seeking to honor God is critical to responsibly evaluating the performance of employees. Handling a performance review with a godly perspective is humbly realizing that we are not the primary judge and arbiter in this regard.

Christ warned us about the judgment and evaluation of others in the Gospel of Matthew:

"Judge not, that you be not judged. For with the judgment you pronounce you will be judged, and with the measure you use it will be measured to you" (Matthew 7:1-2).

Christ is cautioning us to not use our own standard of measurement to evaluate others. If we judge others by our standards, then God uses this same standard to measure us, and we fall short as well. We have failed to show grace and mercy to a sinner like us in need of a savior.

When we judge by our own standards, when we are critical of other's faults, we get a strange sense of superiority over them.

There is a prideful reaction to judging others harshly. If we judge without mercy, we will be judged without mercy by God and men. If we judge with an unkind heart, we will likewise be judged by God and men. This is not Christ's heart toward us (Romans 5:8).

Jesus is also implying that there is no way we can judge the motives of someone's heart, only God can do that.

The only one that can judge the motives of the heart is the only one with a perfect heart, Jesus Christ. God is the first and final judge, we are not. (See Genesis 18:25; Psalm 89:18, 145:17; Habakkuk 1:13.)

Therefore, we are to evaluate others based on a set of standards outside of ourselves. This takes our man-centered opinions and preconceived notions completely out of the equation.

So, how are we to provide feedback or an evaluation to someone if our judgment of the heart is faulty? We need to focus strictly on behavior, actions, and outcomes. That's it. Any attempt to judge or evaluate "why" someone is a certain way, or "why" someone did something, quickly leads us down the road of judging someone's heart motives. We are to evaluate others based on objective, rather than subjective, performance indicators, and the more specific the better.

Take time to read the Parable of the Talents (Matthew 25:14-30; Luke 19:11-27). Jesus' main point in this parable is that we will be judged or evaluated on the faithful use of the talents (or gifts) He has given us to serve in His Kingdom. The results in the parable were quantifiable. Each of the productive servants increased their talents. The lazy servant kept the status quo. The implied expectation of the parable is that the servants were to put the talents to productive use. The lazy or "wicked" servant sought only to protect himself from punishment or wrath and squandered the opportunity. There were negative consequences to this self-protection.

The same principle applies in evaluating the performance of others in the workplace. How did the employee take advantage of the opportunities of his or her employment during the past year to be more productive? What were the quantifiable results? Did they squander the opportunity or make the best use of the gifts and resources that were presented? Here are some practical tips on conducting an employee performance review:

1. Lay the groundwork.

An individual should know in advance what you expect from them in their job. This could be in the form of a job description or simply an agreed-to objective. Meet with the employee and ensure alignment to the expectations. Measure progress throughout the year and provide regular feedback. I would recommend that the more job expectations you can communicate in writing the better. You can actually hold an individual accountable to written expectations. There is little to no ambiguity with written communication.

The feedback of a performance review should not be a surprise. The employee should already know what you think of their performance prior to giving any scheduled performance review. Some would argue that an annual performance review is just a formality, while others say that it's the only time they actually give feedback to an employee. Both of these attitudes miss the mark.

For years, I have regularly scheduled weekly touch points with my direct and indirect reports. This has proven invaluable in talking through workplace issues and how to handle them. I have been able to give them direct and immediate feedback rather than waiting until a performance review to provide it.

This does a few things. If there is an issue that needs to be resolved or obstacles that need to be removed, we can make those course corrections sooner rather than later, before it becomes a much bigger issue.

I am also able to get to know them on a more personal level. Granted, a manager cannot become a close friend because it impacts his or her ability to correct performance issues and provide objective feedback. But getting to know about someone's family or hobbies outside of work is valuable in coaching them through their career. Coaching an individual into a higher level of performance is more than just being a professional career coach. It is understanding an individual's motivations and teaching them how to handle complex workplace situations in the moment rather than after a situation has occurred.

2. Communicate "why."

It's valuable to communicate not only the expectations of the role, but why the role exists. Communicate the productive impact to the department or the organization. Explain the goals that you as their manager are trying to achieve. This gives your employee a sense of purpose within the organization. They are not just a "cog in the wheel" of a company engine. They are valued for their contribution. It also provides a tremendous opportunity for the employee to offer a better way to accomplish the goal or, better yet, exceed the goal. Explaining the end goal and purpose of the role empowers the employee to contribute to the best of their ability and to seek continuous improvement.

3. Pray before the review.

It's important that you ask God what He would like to have you communicate to this employee and how to present it. An experienced manager will tend to rely on experience and previous expectations, but God's picture is certainly bigger than ours (Isaiah 55:8). Also pray that you maintain a godly, humble attitude throughout the review and feedback, regardless of the employee's reactions (Philippians 2:3-4).

4. Invest the time.

Good employees sincerely want to know how you believe they have performed this year. They place tremendous weight on your evaluation. Be humbled by this. Most employees sincerely desire to do good work and strive to meet your expectations. Devote the appropriate time to this exercise, don't just make it a formal "check-the-box" event. It should be a professional dialogue between the manager and employee. Good employees respond positively when you invest the time to express a sincere interest in their personal and professional growth.

5. Communicate organizational health first.

Be sure that your employees understand the financial status of the organization and their impact on it. If the organization is struggling financially, then your employees need to know where, how, and why. If the organization is doing well, how has the employee contributed to the success? How can this success be sustained or even improved upon? It would not be appropriate to share specific financial data, yet you can typically provide a high-level picture and outlook.

6. Give the performance rating and wage decisions up front.

I understand that there are two schools of thought here: first or last. I have always provided this up front. This is the bottom-line for employees and most are just wading through the rest of the performance discussion to get there. I get it out of the way first and then we discuss the rationalization or justification for the decision. Although the review itself is important supporting information to convey, this is the primary information that your employees will use to determine your perception of their performance.

7. Use specific examples.

Be sure and provide specific areas where an individual did well and could have done better. Use numerical data whenever possible. Use facts and specific examples to support your position.

8. Remain appropriately objective.

Control any emotions you might feel during the performance review. Emotions only escalate an issue in a negative direction. It is not productive. Don't react to the employee's emotions. If an employee reacts negatively or becomes upset, stick to the specific facts. "You did well here . . . not so well here." Communicate why they underperformed. Use specific examples and previously communicated expectations. If they continue to be upset, it might be necessary to reschedule the meeting for another time.

9. This is not about you!

I hesitate to say this, but it needs to be said. In the same vein as remaining objective, the goals for the employee should be about making the organization or department better, not to meet your personal, self-defined, or biased expectations. Your employees are not there to meet your personal needs. Your expectations should directly align with the organization or department's objectives. Sincerely evaluate your own heart: Are you being objective in this regard?

10. Be honest.

If an employee is behind in his or her performance, be honest. The only way an individual is going to improve is that they know where they need to improve. I have seen too many managers who are afraid of a difficult conversation or simply do not know how to have one.

11. Look to the future.

Provide feedback but focus on future organizational or individual goals for the next year. This is an opportunity for you to communicate the organization's future objectives and to align on your expectations for the role in the coming year.

12. Learn the employee's career goals.

These could change from year to year. Knowing your employee's professional and personal goals is the best way to coach them to success. This may also provide an opportunity to draft a development plan for the employee.

13. Follow up.

If necessary, do a follow-up. Sometimes an employee needs time to process feedback. Set a reasonable time to get back together and discuss next steps for you and the employee.

14. Encourage regular communication after the review.

Be available when an employee has an issue that they want to run by you for your opinion or recommendation. This is an excellent coaching opportunity for the individual and is necessary for their development. It also avoids future (or bigger) problems. Don't immediately resolve the issue. Give them the opportunity to do that on their own.

Performance Review Traps

I want to make you aware of certain performance review traps that I have seen many managers fall into. Search your heart and ask God to reveal if you currently are susceptible to any of these performance review missteps.

Recency – Don't measure someone based on their most recent performance. An employee could be performing poorly all year but two weeks before their performance review, their productivity skyrockets. Measure the employee for the whole period. Employees know when review time comes around.

Halo effect – Sometimes an employee is so good in many areas that managers ignore the employee's lack of performance in others and fails to address them.

Stereotyping – Don't stereotype individuals based on historical or perceived generalizations or stereotypes. Measure and give feedback on the individual's performance. For example, you might have a stereotype that men make better construction contractors than women, or women make better customer service representatives than men. Evaluate an individual's performance to the job expectations of the role.

Soft-pedal approach – Some managers rate all their employees exceedingly high regardless of performance or team productivity. This is just a way of avoiding difficult conversations or confronting an employee's poor performance. Some managers rationalize this avoidance by arguing that encouragement, praise, and a higher rating is the only thing that motivates their employees. They argue that negative feedback is a demotivation for their team. However, they fail to recognize that employees need direct feedback to correct and resolve poor performance. Failure to communicate directly to a poor performer inhibits the employee's growth and stifles team productivity and morale.

Hard-pedal approach – Conversely, some managers will never give good ratings. They falsely believe a low rating keeps employees from thinking too highly of themselves. They rationalize that this will motivate employees to perform better or produce more. This only demoralizes the individual team members. Good employees do not remain in a hyper-critical environment for long.

These are the most common employee performance evaluation traps that managers fall into. While there could be more, simply remember these two key points:

1. Individual ratings should reflect individual performance.

How did the individual perform based on his or her pre-determined goals for the year? Don't punish your best performers because your poor performers caused your team to miss productivity goals. If you are able and have the budget, recognize their efforts. If you cannot because the financial productivity was too damaging, seek an exception or communicate this message not only to the individual, but to the entire team.

2. Team ratings should reflect team performance.

If your team did not meet productivity goals, then your overall ratings should reflect this. While some individuals might have performed very well despite the team's overall productivity, not everyone did. There should be a direct correlation between your overall individual employee performance ratings and your team's productivity. If you have appropriately aligned your individual performance goals with the team productivity goals, then your overall ratings would reflect this.

An employee's performance review is something that we should give adequate credence and preparation in presenting. We owe this to our employees. In doing so, we honor God with the authority that He has granted us.

For Further Study

1. Read 2 Samuel 12:1-7. What was Samuel doing in relating the story of one man stealing another man's ewe? How was David's judgment condemning himself?

2. Read Genesis 18:17-27. What counsel did Moses receive in regard to choosing judges over the people?

3. Do you get pleasure or a feeling of superiority in pointing out another individual's faults?

Chapter 7

Receiving a Negative Performance Review

One of the hardest things for us to do is humble ourselves to the point of listening when people are pointing out our failures or inadequacies (or their perception of them). But learning how to do this in a consistent and godly way is critical to our spiritual growth. God's loving sovereignty regularly places us in a position to practice this humility, one of which could be a review of our job performance.

In the course of our employment, we are faced with negative feedback at one time or another. This is a normal part of the working world in which we live. Most of this positive or negative reaction comes during a scheduled job performance review. The details of the performance evaluation may or may not be factual and we may even disagree with the message. It may even be a deliberate attempt to falsely accuse us of poor performance to discredit us, but then again there may be some truth to the message that we need to hear. We need to be open to this. The accuracy of facts or perceptions can be addressed at a more appropriate time if necessary. The most critical thing during a performance review is the initial reaction and response. Now, some of you may never, or rarely, receive any type of formal job performance review. It may be more of an informal or "spur of the moment" discussion. The setting or format doesn't matter. What matters is that your initial response will quickly reveal your desire or ability to receive correction.

Many proverbs speak to this biblical principle, one of which is Proverbs 5:12-13:

> *"How I hated discipline, and my heart despised reproof! I did not listen to the voice of my teachers or incline my ear to my instructors."*

In applying this concept to our workplace, we must first identify the reason we resist instruction and correction. We naturally resist or hate instruction and spurn reproof because of our prideful, sinful hearts. We will also ignore, devalue, or minimize the instruction we are given to justify our rebellion. In following our own wisdom and passions, we eventually find ourselves in a dire situation. Such is the case in Proverbs 5.

In the practical application of receiving workplace instruction, we must remember that our role at work is not to do things our own way and in our own wisdom. We are to submit to and follow the direction of our God-ordained leaders. They have certain expectations of our performance, and we are to make every effort to meet and exceed those expectations, whether we agree with them or not (Romans 13:1). Now obviously, this does not apply to illegal or immoral direction. That is another discussion topic, and is normally not the case. There are respectful ways to challenge leadership and there are times when it is totally appropriate to do so, but not during a performance review. If you find yourself on the receiving end of a poor performance review, remember these key things:

1. Listen!

Don't immediately interrupt with defensive or corrective reactions. Our first response will be to either defend ourselves or perhaps become despondent. Resist any immediate reaction to the moment and entrust yourself to Him who judges justly (Psalm 118:8-9; 1 Peter 2:23). Be quick to hear and slow to speak (James 1:19-20), even if insulted (Matthew 5:39). I encourage you to take notes of the discussion for future reference.

2. Don't lose perspective.

Don't take it so personally that you forget that you belong to Christ. Taking criticism personally becomes a self-focused attitude as well. You have not lost your identity in Christ. Just because we may have some things to work on or change doesn't make us less precious to Christ. Becoming emotional to the point of sadness or anxiety is not God-honoring or glorifying to His sacrifice. It is not trusting His sovereign, sanctifying work in our lives (Psalm 23; Philippians 4:6-7).

3. Ask for specifics.

Ask clarifying questions and request specific examples. It is completely appropriate to ask questions of your manager to clarify his or her position and request specific examples of what is missing in your performance, such as, "Can you give me an example of when I didn't finish the job properly?"

4. Resolve to do excellent work.

Reinforce your desire to meet the expectations of your position. However, it is important to remember that we are honoring Christ in our work, over and above our manager (Ephesians 6:5-8; Colossians 3:23-24). God is not glorified when we work to our own standard or minimally to our employer's standards. We are to do excellent work and exceed expectations to glorify Him and be a witness of His gospel.

5. Correct inaccuracies respectfully and humbly.

It is very appropriate to correct inaccurate information at the appropriate time. If you happen to be proven correct, don't react pridefully. If you behave as if you've "beaten your boss at his or her own game" you will end up losing support in the long run (Proverbs 16:18; Philippians 2:1-11; 1 Peter 2:23).

6. Don't expect to have a godly attitude right away.

This will take some time to process. Earnestly pray, then pray even more! Seek out godly counsel if necessary. If you did react negatively in any way, apologize for it.

7. Change what you need to change.

Don't ignore and minimize the expectations or opinions given. Receive the correction and make every effort to correct and improve your performance. Ask your manager on a regular basis if you are on track. "How am I doing since we talked?"

8. Expect consequences if you react negatively or refuse to make changes.

This could mean being passed up for a promotion, not selected for special projects, or eventual termination. There needs to be a healthy fear of consequences to our prideful actions that would encourage us to listen and heed the words of those in authority as these behaviors are ultimately opposing the very ordinance of God (Proverbs 1:7, 16:18; Romans 13:1-7; Ephesians 6:5-8).

I have witnessed and given many performance reviews in which the employee reacts poorly to this discussion and never learns the lesson of submitting to an employer's expectations. It becomes a constant battle between the employee and employer and one that the employee usually loses. I have also witnessed employees who accept reproof with a humble heart and spirit, who learn from the correction and make every effort to meet and exceed their employer's expectations with regular meetings and requests for feedback (Colossians 3:23-24). (Review Chapter 4: "Difficult Boss Relationship.") They end up being extraordinarily successful in developing positive working relationships and honoring God with their attitude.

A defensive, un-submissive, and hard heart sends a strong message that you are not interested in anyone's correction or instruction and believe your own wisdom is superior (1 Corinthians 1:20-21; James 3:13-18). Why would a boss or an organization invest time, effort, or a future in anyone with this attitude? It is impossible for a prideful and un-submissive person to learn anything, and it is equally impossible for a person with this attitude to submit to and receive godly direction and correction. This should be a sobering reminder to all of us. A willing desire to receive instruction and correction is the first step to honoring, and even understanding, God's loving instruction and correction.

For Further Study

1. Read Proverbs 5. What were the consequences of hating and spurning instruction in this passage?

2. In what ways do we devalue or minimize instruction?

3. Read 1 Corinthians 1: 18-25. Why do many resist the message of the gospel? How does this relate to resisting instruction?

4. Do we have the right to not consider the instruction of unbelievers? Read 1 Peter 2:18-25. How is submission related to receiving instruction?

Chapter 8

Receiving a Good Performance Review

I was given a positive performance review because of a year of dedicated work to achieving my employer's goals and objectives. I was extremely proud of the recognition of this work. So, I committed to delivering a similar performance the next year. At the end of the year, I believed I had delivered even better results than the previous year. I went into my annual review expecting to be praised and rewarded in a similar fashion. I was not. It was received as simply meeting the expectations of the role. I was extremely disappointed. I felt like I deserved a better annual rating than just meeting expectations. After all, I had already proven my worth and was continuing down the same path. This resulted in an attitude of resentment and bitterness toward my boss and employer. I was obviously not working to please God, but to please men and boost my ego (Colossians 3:23).

Our response to a positive performance review is just as critical as our reaction to a negative one. We must keep a godly focus during and after this message. The passage I want to bring to mind may be a little bit of a surprise to some:

> *"But now the righteousness of God has been manifested apart from the law, although the Law and the Prophets bear witness to it— the righteousness of God through faith in Jesus Christ for all who believe. For there is no distinction: for all have sinned and fall short of the glory of God, and are justified by his grace as a gift, through the redemption that is in Christ Jesus, whom God put forward as a propitiation by his blood, to be received by faith.*
>
> *This was to show God's righteousness, because in his divine forbearance he had passed over former sins. It was to show his righteousness at the present time, so that he might be just and the justifier of the one who has faith in Jesus. Then what becomes of our boasting? It is excluded. By what kind of law? By a law of works? No, but by the law of faith." (Romans 3:21-27)*

Paul's message to the Roman church is that there is no way that we can fulfill the Law adequately enough to please God and cover our sin. We all fall short in this attempt. Only through our faith in Christ can we be justified freely through His redemptive grace. But this attitude of working harder and longer to achieve a reward, a goal, or to be pleasing to men (and even God) is embedded in our nature and is manifested in an obvious way when we react pridefully to a positive performance review.

We think we deserve a reward such as more pay, a promotion, recognition, or continued favorable employment when we work hard. God determines what we deserve. In God's economy, we deserve eternal separation from Him. We all fall short. Our good work performance is empty and void compared to God's holiness.

We do not deserve or earn the loving grace of our salvation by anything we do or achieve. We must maintain that same attitude when God in His sovereignty grants us a positive performance review in the course of our employment, we don't deserve it. We receive positive performance reviews to glorify God and celebrate His handiwork in our life.

So, considering this, how do we respond?

1. Practice humility.

Augustine once said that the three key principles of the Christian religion "is first humility, second humility, third humility" (see Philippians 2:3-8). There will be an immediate reaction to be prideful of a good performance review and attempt to reaffirm this viewpoint during the meeting. Resist this urge. It only becomes a self-serving but futile attempt to gain glory that should be God directed.

2. Thank your boss for the support.

Your boss is obviously pleased with your performance and can continue to be a supporter and advocate of you in the future. Be sure to express gratitude.

3. Don't boast.

Don't boast to others about your positive review (Proverbs 15:33; 1 Corinthians13:4-5; James 3:5). This only alienates your peers and co-workers and again, is an attempt to build yourself up rather than acknowledging God's sovereignty. You will not be a godly witness of humility as you share the gospel message. Your next one may not be as positive.

4. Don't treat others as inferior.

First of all, this isn't true. We are all sinners, (including the one who just received a good performance review). Treating others as inferior only alienates your co-workers and damages your credibility as a Christian (Philippians 2:3-4).

5. Continue to look for ways to improve.

Ask your manager how you can get even better. This displays an attitude of humility in recognizing that you are not perfect and still have areas that need improvement.

6. Look for ways to mentor others to improve their work.

Intentionally make the effort to pass on your experience and knowledge. This will be appreciated more than you know. It may even open doors to share why you work the way you do and, more importantly, share the gospel.

7. Praise and be grateful to God.

Be quick to remember that the skills and abilities that allowed you to receive this positive performance review and even the ability to earn a living are directly from God Himself. You contributed nothing to this (Exodus 31:6; Deuteronomy 8:16-18). Praise God that He has given you this opportunity of increased credibility and the opening of doors with others in the workplace to be a godly witness and proclaim the gospel.

If we are truly working to please God rather than people, we will recognize that the outcome of a positive or negative performance review is divinely orchestrated to glorify God and proclaim His Kingdom, not to further our own standard of living or bolster our ego. This may manifest itself in several ways, but humility is the common denominator. Remembering God's holiness, His sovereignty over the hearts of kings (Proverbs 21:1; Daniel 2:21), and His sanctifying love in our lives will help us maintain an attitude of humility in either outcome.

For Further Study

1. If you are overly consumed with the receipt of a good performance review, where is your focus? (1 John 2:16)

2. Read Proverbs 29:25. How can a good performance review be a snare?

3. Read Philippians 3:3-11. What had Paul accomplished in his life? To what did he compare his good performance and achievements, considering the knowledge of Christ?

4. Read 2 Peter 1:5-8. Where should we be focusing our time and energy of continuous improvement? Why?

Chapter 9

Managing Poor Performance

I n my Human Resources role, I frequently have the unfortunate task of either addressing underperforming employees directly or counseling managers to address employee performance. Understanding how to address underperforming employees from a biblical perspective is different than simply following an organizational process of discipline or, conversely, turning a blind eye to ungodly behavior or poor performance out of "patience and love." There is a loving balance between accountability and mercy that we are to seek in addressing most of the employee performance issues you will deal with.

Employees who struggle in their work performance fall into several different categories for a variety of reasons. A single-formula approach to every situation rarely achieves the desired result, which is to have an employee who meets or exceeds the expectations of the role. Some specific instances of poor performance could include:

- An employee refuses to perform the job per his manager's direction.

- A struggling employee has a sincere desire to do the job well but just doesn't have the skill-set required for the role.
- A long-term employee may be unusually negligent while going through a difficult personal situation.
- An employee is blatantly insubordinate, or constantly berating and abusive to co-workers and management.

Many managers hesitate to confront poor performers or, when they do, go from "zero to sixty" in addressing the poor performance, ineffectively swinging the pendulum from one extreme to the other. These managers typically make some attempt to work with the employee behind the scenes, but to no avail. This only results in frustration for both the employee and the manager.

The manager will then contact Human Resources in exasperation, stating, "They aren't getting it and we just need to let them go." This is not the correct course of action. There are federal and state laws that ensure a fair and equitable workplace for all employees. Unless this employee has deliberately violated the law or specific company policy, it is never advisable to immediately terminate a poorly performing employee without a proper investigation and/ or a consistent and deliberate attempt to correct the behavior.

However, there are times where immediate termination is warranted and even advisable. Usually those are cases where a criminal law was broken or incidents that require an immediate response from the organization to avoid negative repercussions or even legal action if not addressed. These incidents are rare. Your corporate attorney or Human Resources contact can provide the proper guidance in these situations.

Often, struggling employees simply need to be encouraged and know that you, as their manager, are on their side and invested in their success. Make every effort to provide them with all the training, tools, and resources necessary for them to succeed. Encourage them to excel still more in their efforts. Reward and praise them at significant milestones of success.

Knowing how and when to apply each of these management techniques is sometimes a difficult balance. But if a manager is skilled at this, his team will consistently meet, or exceed, productivity goals and even reach out to others to train and encourage them to do excellent work.

One passage of Scripture that has always been helpful to me in how to approach employee performance issues from a practical and biblical perspective is 1 Thessalonians 5:14-15:

> *"And we urge you, brothers, admonish the idle, encourage the fainthearted, help the weak, be patient with them all. See that no one repays anyone evil for evil, but always seek to do good to one another and to everyone."*

In this passage, Paul is specifically addressing the church of Thessalonica as he directs the behavior of the church body to one another. But, in verse 15, he encourages them to extend the seeking of good to all people. This also applies to unbelievers. These guidelines help us apply biblical concepts to the behavior of anyone who is unruly, fainthearted, or weak. Paul recognizes the need for varying approaches to people at different points in their lives and in different circumstances. Let's break this passage down a little before we discuss some practical application.

Paul is "urging" the Thessalonians to address the following issues sooner rather than later. "Urge" is from the Greek word *parakaleo*, which means "to come alongside," and gives the idea of providing help to someone. This is not beating someone into a type of submission. Rather this is a counseling or coaching to help someone become better.

Paul urges them to admonish, or warn, the unruly. The unruly are those that are not in sync with the way that things are to be done. This is the idea of alerting someone of the dire consequences that lie ahead if they pursue their current direction.

He then urges the Thessalonians to encourage the fainthearted. The Greek word for "fainthearted" literally means "small souled." The fainthearted lack the boldness to sustain adversity. They are people who seek safety and security and are risk averse. Fainthearted people need encouragement to stand firm in the face of a challenge, to be bold in what they know is right.

Helping the weak is a command for the stronger believers to come alongside and work together with those that are weaker, to develop close personal relationships with them and provide instruction and training in righteous behavior. Paul then urges the church to "be patient with everyone." This patience is filled with long-suffering and forgiveness for those that are "different" from us (1 Corinthians 13:4-7).

Hand in hand with this patience and forgiveness is resisting the urge to retaliate against those who have wronged us or others. There is no place for personal vengeance toward anyone regardless of the sin committed. We are to seek their good, that which is best for them - a good that is pure, noble, and excellent (Philippians 4:8). That is the passage in its context.

I know that applying this passage to the workplace sounds complex, but it's simple if you patiently seek to understand the heart of the behavior rather than treat each person and situation the same way every time.

You will address a poor performer who is insubordinate differently than one who simply has not been trained to properly do the job. One employee has no motivation or desire to do excellent work while the other may have the desire but not the skill-set. Here are some helpful hints:

1. Don't ignore the poor performer.

If there are individuals on your team who are not meeting expectations, you may be the type of manager who has a tendency to avoid the difficult conversation secretly hoping the performance will miraculously get better. It very rarely does. Your team sees the poor performer and is watching how you handle the situation. Failing to address the underperformer only sends the message that a poor level of performance is tolerated. This will eventually lower the overall performance and morale of your team.

2. Seek to understand the reason for the poor performance.

It may be a "submission to authority" issue, a personal issue at home, a lack of the proper skill-set, or a lack of sufficient training. The reason(s) for the poor performance doesn't negate the need to address the issue, but it will change your approach.

3. Confirm the disciplinary issue(s) that need to be addressed.

This may sound redundant, but there have been many cases where I confronted an employee and found out that I had incomplete or incorrect information. Use the Matthew 18 principle with the purpose of gathering facts from the individual, verifying with another manager (or even a previous manager), and then taking the necessary action based on first-hand and factual knowledge. As in the case of Matthew 18, some of the more serious meetings will need a witness or managerial support to address the issue (Matthew 18:15-17).

4. Don't use empathy as an excuse to avoid performance issues.

This is admittedly a tough one and an easy trap to fall into. I have worked with many managers (primarily Christians) who, with good intentions and a sympathetic heart, hesitate to address poor performance to avoid being viewed as "hard hearted" and "calloused." They believe that holding a struggling employee accountable doesn't honor Christ's love, mercy, and grace. On the contrary, Christ confronted ungodly behavior but still displayed and expressed love for those He confronted. You can be sympathetic and come alongside the employee up to a certain point, but accommodating the employee long-term will eventually have a negative impact on the individual and your team. There are many organizational benefits for employees going through difficult personal situations and training programs for employees who lack the appropriate skill-set. Your job as a leader is to point them to these benefits and programs and hold them accountable to their response, not to reduce your performance standards. Failing to address poor performance in response to an individual's personal situation is a slippery slope that only gets worse with time. Eventually everyone has personal situations that affect their work. Finding that balance between empathy and accountability is a leader's responsibility.

5. Don't respond harshly.

I used to work with a manager whose mantra was "the beatings will continue until morale improves." It's a witty saying, but not an effective tactic. I have witnessed many managers who are quick to respond to underperforming employees with a heavy hand and attempt to "brow beat" them into meeting performance expectations. They are quick to present them with documented disciplinary action without fully understanding the reasons that contribute to this behavior. This is a terribly de-motivating management style and one that ultimately breaks down a team. The manager eventually loses all support.

6. Maintain objectivity.

Refrain from being overly sympathetic or overly harsh and even angry. Poor performing employees may elicit an emotional reaction from you as the manager. Maybe you feel badly for the employee, or maybe you have lost your patience and are tired of tolerating the poor performance of this employee. Remain steady and focused. Keep the conversation on work-related issues and provide factual responses to how an employee is failing to meet the expectations of the role. Don't react to the employee's emotions. They could respond by crying or becoming angry and defensive. Be prepared for an emotional response but don't react to it. Emotional reactions tend to escalate things. Take proactive steps to maintain your composure. Prepare yourself for this.

7. Keep the message of the gospel in the forefront of any action you take.

There is a short-term objective to addressing employee performance but an even more important long-term desire for all to come into a relationship with Christ. This is the key to determining the biblical path of addressing under-performers. Paul's intent in the passage above was to address these individuals in a way that confronted their sin but pointed them toward the goodness of the gospel and the message of eternal life. If you maintain a gospel mindset, mercy and grace is the primary focus when addressing every individual, regardless of their behavior. If you keep an eternal perspective in mind and address them as Christ would, this impacts your actions. Don't let a fixation on short-term objectives harden your heart to Christ's mission.

I have developed the chart below as a general guideline, but always consult with your manager, Human Resources, or an Employee Relations specialist before you take any action.

Performance Issue
Willful disregard of job expectations
Reason: Failure to submit to authority
Action: Communicate the expectations of the role via a job description and specific aspects that they are not meeting. Document the conversation.
Outcome: Failure to submit to the expectations of the role becomes a performance issue subject to formal disciplinary action and could lead to termination.

Performance Issue
Performance suddenly drops from previously good or excellent work.
Reason: Personal issue at home (e.g., divorce, sickness, etc.)
Action: You should display empathy, but you must still stress the need for the employee to address the gaps in performance related to the expectations of the role. Recommend your organization's Employee Assistance Program (EAP) if you have one. If not, recommend that the employee get outside help to deal with the issue. Don't attempt to provide any medical or professional counseling advice to the situation. This is not your role, and you could put the organization at legal risk. However, you can direct them to professional help.

> **Outcome:** Even if an individual is going through a difficult personal situation, you as a manager can and should express empathy, but the ultimate responsibility still lies with the employee and the performance will still need to be addressed. A failure by the employee to address gaps in performance will be subject to a disciplinary action and process.

Performance Issue
Lack of skill-set to meet the expectations (general or specific) of the current role.

Reason: Inability to perform the role due to a lack of training, physical limitations, or education

Action: First identify which specific skill-set is lacking, such as computer skills, selling skills, organizational skills, etc. Determine the best method/ training appropriate to improve the skill-set.

Outcome: Provide an opportunity for training or retraining on the specific skills lacking. Give a time frame to achieve competency. Failing to achieve competency by this pre-determined time frame will result in the need to proceed through the performance management process. Perhaps a different role may be considered for the employee.

Terminating an Employee

At one time, I was the Human Resources Manager for a food manufacturing plant. One day, some employees complained that a co-worker was often taking bags of damaged food product home with him. This employee was bagging food product from refrigerated areas of damaged goods that employees could draw from only for their lunch breaks. This was considered theft of product according to company policy.

The employee in question had experienced a stroke a few years earlier, and had difficulty obtaining gainful employment or understanding complex job responsibilities. This job was a blessing for him. When confronted, he confessed that he was not aware that he was doing anything wrong and humbly apologized. He stated that he was not willfully trying to steal product. I terminated him anyway. He came in a few days later asking me to reconsider. His family believed that termination of his employment was too harsh. I held firm. I think of this situation often now that I am a Christian. I still remember his name and face. This is one of my many regrets at missing an opportunity to show grace and mercy to someone who needed it. In retrospect, if I had followed the guidelines above, the situation would more than likely had rectified itself. I was too harsh.

Depending on the circumstances and your specific company policies, there will be situations that result in immediate termination (i.e., violation of federal or state law, theft, physical altercations, safety violations, substance abuse, etc.). There are also times where employees either cannot or will not respond to any correction and the result is termination. Remember to handle these with grace and patience as well. A terminated employee will suffer severe personal consequences for their actions. If you handle the situation with a hard heart or harsh attitude, God is not glorified.

Here are just a few practical things to consider in preparation for an employee termination. These guidelines are obviously not all inclusive. Every situation is different and poses its own set of risks. This is not legal advice. You must refer to your HR or Legal Department for your next steps.

1. Maintain detailed and accurate documentation.

This is important in case the termination is challenged.

2. Ensure that all necessary parties are on board.

Your immediate manager, Human Resources, and your legal department should be involved. If not, understand the risk that you are assuming.

3. Be brief.
There is no need to revisit previous discussions or documentation. This only confuses the issue.

4. Don't react to the terminated employee's emotions.
This only escalates the issue.

5. There may be times where a public place or a police presence is necessary.
If the employee has exhibited erratic behavior in the past or you believe that the physical safety of you or others is a serious concern, consider professional protection.

6. Be considerate of the timing.
Don't time the termination of someone to avoid paying them some type of compensation (e.g., end of the year bonus, vacation, etc.).

7. Keep everything confidential.
Do not disclose the reasons for termination to their co-workers or to anyone else.

I have often wondered on what basis do leaders in certain organization address underperforming individuals. What is their compass or source of reason? I have found that some leaders confront behavior and performance based on the policies set forth by the organization, some by specific job descriptions and expectations, and some confront based on their own personal agenda.

As a believer, I have the wisdom of the Holy Spirit living within me. This is my compass and my source of truth. This is what I rely on to get to the "sin-root" of underperforming employees.

Be a leader that understands the balance between holding individuals accountable to job performance while maintaining a focus on Christ's desire for them: eternal life and Christlike behavior. Let your commitment to Christ and His mission guide your steps to addressing underperforming employees.

For Further Study

1. Read John 4:1-38. How did Jesus confront the sin and what was His guidance?
2. Read Luke 11: 37-53. How is this passage different than the passage above, and why?
3. Would you ever use this approach?
4. How did Christ "manage" His disciples? Give scriptural examples.

Chapter 10

Conducting an Interview

Searching for and hiring the right employee is difficult work. The costs of hiring a bad employee are impossible to gauge, and could result in bad morale, poor management, declining productivity, or worse.

What do you look for in an employee? Technical skills? Education? Experience? Work history? Yes! All these factors need to be taken into consideration depending on the position you are looking to fill.

But, ultimately, the practical, day-to-day application of an individual's skill-set and education is the key to hiring a good employee. There is only one metric that can tie all these things together: a godly character. You can have all the knowledge, experience, and education that the world has to offer but improper application of that skill-set nullifies it.

One of my favorite passages of Scripture is found in 1 Samuel 16 when the Lord directs Samuel to search for a new king of Israel to replace Saul. Saul had sinned against the Lord and sought to please men rather than obey God. God instructed Samuel to travel to Bethlehem and meet with Jesse, the father of eight sons. As the sons of Jesse entered the room, Samuel's eyes immediately fell on Eliab and he thought, "Surely the Lord's anointed is before Him."

> *"But the Lord said to Samuel, "Do not look on his appearance or on the height of his stature, because I have rejected him. For the Lord sees not as man sees: man looks on the outward appearance, but the Lord looks on the heart." (1 Samuel 16:7)*

One by one, Jesse proudly paraded his sons before Samuel, each one rejected by God. Jesse did not even bring his youngest in for consideration, as he was not old enough to be eligible (in Jesse's eyes). However, the youngest was David. And, when it was requested that Jesse present David, Samuel was instructed by God to anoint him the next king of Israel. God chose a man with the right character to lead Israel, a man after God's own heart.

Don't get me wrong; having the right technical skill and experience to do the job is vitally important. Someone could have the right heart but not the right skill-set to do the job, and that would still be a bad choice. But the final decision to hire should lie in how they practically apply their knowledge and experience.

There are many ways to interview applicants for a position. Screening out those who do not meet the minimum experience or skills is an appropriate first step.

What are some interviewing techniques to gather information on an applicant's character?

1. Ask questions that require the candidate to give real-life examples.

This is the key to identifying how they would work. How they handled specific issues in the past will reveal how they will handle future workplace issues. For instance, invite them to describe a time where they were asked to violate company policy. What was the situation, how did they respond, and what was the result? If you want to know if they have a drive for results, ask them to describe a time where they were put into a situation to meet lofty productivity goals. What was the situation, how did they respond, and what was the result? As Scripture reminds us, the proof is in the "fruit of the Spirit" (Galatians 5:22-23).

2. Be a detective.

Continue drilling down until you get specific answers to all of the questions above. How they resolved the issue is just as important as getting the job done. Also, don't just take their word for it. I learned that during one particular interview. A candidate stated that he had a certain skill-set necessary for the job, but after hiring it was revealed that he misrepresented himself. Further questioning or proof of certifications would have uncovered this gap.

3. Have they done their due diligence?

The first question I ask a candidate I am interviewing is, "What do you know about us?" If they respond with some details about who we are as an organization and what we stand for, then I know they have done their research and are interested in working for our organization. I have had many candidates respond with "not much." This tells me several things. For one, it tells me they have not bothered to research the company or position and therefore they possess little passion for the role or the organization. The interview becomes a formality at that point.

4. Do not ask personal questions that would uncover information that is deemed as discriminatory.

Failure to hire based on an individual's race, gender, religion, national origin, veteran status, or disability is against federal law. There are individual states that add classifications to this list as well; be aware of them. Do not ask leading questions that would reveal this information (e.g., When did you graduate high school? Do you have any children? What religion are you?). If the candidate offers any of this information voluntarily, don't respond or ask follow-up questions. Do not note this information for use in the selection process.

5. Do ask questions regarding the specific duties and responsibilities of the role.

Are you able to work the schedule as required? Is there anything that would prevent you from fulfilling the duties and responsibilities the position requires?

6. There are some personal questions that you can ask.

What management style do you work best under? What is your management style? What do you do to relieve stress? What are your passions? This conversation will reveal more about the person than just speaking to technical skills. You would be surprised what you can learn about an individual when they are asked to describe what passions they have. Perhaps they love to volunteer at a local orphanage or homeless shelter, or they are active in their church, or love to just sit and binge-watch TV every weekend, or even participate in Triathlons. This gives you an idea for their value system.

7. Check out social media.

It amazes me what some folks post on their social media accounts. While you cannot disqualify a candidate for their personal life, you can certainly get an idea about their core behavior and values and determine if they align with what they have told you in the interview.

8. Conduct an appropriate background check.

A background check provides key insights into a future employee's character. At times, it will reveal a discrepancy on a resume or application that, if intentional, would be considered falsifying documents. It could also uncover a criminal record that may disqualify them from certain roles and responsibilities (e.g., an embezzlement conviction when being considered for a role in accounting). Be careful with this; a criminal record alone will not disqualify an individual, according to some federal and state laws. Other times a background check will reveal a changed and repentant life.

9. Remember, not everyone is a Christian.

Don't make the mistake that of thinking that every good employee aligns with your Christian values. If you do, you will often be disappointed. There are many solid and contributing potential employees that have an upright and honest character. Your potential employees must display a moral ethical compass and behave in that regard. Even though individuals are not believers, the work of the Law is written on their hearts. (See Romans 2:14-15.)

10. Pray for God's guidance.

Don't rely on your own wisdom alone; seek God's guidance on whom He has prepared for this position. As Samuel learned, God has already selected the perfect candidate for the role. Ask Him whom He would have you hire.

While these are not "fool-proof" methods to hire the most successful candidate, they can provide a framework in determining work ethic and character. I will also recommend working closely with your manager, Human Resources, or Legal Department prior to making any offers of employment to ensure consistency and adherence to federal and state laws.

For Further Study

1. Read 1 Samuel 16. Is this how you would have selected a new king over Israel? What will you consider the next time you hire?

2. Read Acts 1: 15-26. What is happening in this passage? Why was this method chosen? Did God honor this method? Why or why not?

3. Read Galatians 5:22-23. How can you tailor an interview to reveal these attributes?

4. Have you ever hired someone who later was not the right fit? What did you do differently the next time?

Chapter 11

Being Interviewed

Being interviewed for a new job can be one of the most nerve-racking work-related events we can experience. There is a tremendous feeling of vulnerability, as we are giving someone the permission to evaluate and even judge our work experience, character, and personality. We are revealing to a complete stranger everything that gives us any type of worldly value. We reveal past decisions we have made (good and bad) and even past decisions of former bosses and employers. If we are not selected for the role, we tend to let this impact our pride and ego.

The ultimate thing to remember as we prepare for a job interview is God's sovereign hand. Proverbs reminds us that God can move the hearts of kings to grant you a position that can achieve His good purposes (or not), for the same good reasons:

> *"The king's heart is a stream of water in the hand of the Lord; he turns it wherever he will" (Proverbs 21:1).*

Trusting in God's good love for you and what He knows is best is the primary focus of this issue. I must admit that my lack of trust in God's sovereignty is the source of all my anxiety over my circumstances and worry about future events. This has been a sanctifying lesson that God continues to teach me. He has always been faithful to His promises and His character, regardless of whether the outcome is to my liking or not (Genesis 50:20; 2 Chronicles 20:6; Psalm 115:3; Proverbs 16:9). However, there are practical aspects of a job interview that we can consider as well.

Being interviewed can be a struggle for believers in a spiritual sense. We awkwardly feel like we are pridefully inflating ourselves to get a job that we desire. This is completely against the grain of the character of humility that the Christian walk espouses. But though we can certainly make it out to be that way, we don't have to.

The best way to overcome this is to not make the interview about yourself. Make it about the organization with which you are interviewing. What are its needs for the role? How can you best serve and meet those needs? The best way to communicate this is how you have serviced organizational needs in the past, and the result of that service. The attitude to maintain during an interview is reflected in Proverbs:

> *"Let another praise you, and not your own mouth; a stranger, and not your own lips" (Proverbs 27:2).*

You may be saying, "Okay, now that really doesn't make any sense. You *have* to talk about yourself and your accomplishments during an interview." Yes and no. There is a subtle difference here. The word "praise" refers to self-edification. Matthew Henry explains it this way:

"We must do that which is commendable, for which even strangers may praise us. Our light must shine before men, and we must do good works that may be seen, though we must not do them on purpose that they may be seen. Let our own works be such as will praise us, even in the gates, when we have done it we must not commend ourselves, for that is an evidence of pride, folly, and self-love, and a great lessening to a man's reputation. Everyone will be forward to run him down that cries himself up. There may be a just occasion for us to vindicate ourselves, but it does not become us to applaud ourselves. *Proprio laus sordet in ore* ('self-praise defiles the mouth')" [6]

What Henry is saying is that our works speak for themselves. We don't promote ourselves or our successes. Let God promote His own good works. He is ultimately responsible for their success anyway.

So, to refrain from self-edification in a job interview, I would encourage you to just state the facts. For example, use the script below when discussing your work experience and history:

- What was the work challenge or issue you were trying to resolve?
- What steps did you and your team take to resolve the issue or problem?
- How did you come to that conclusion? (Did you use historical data or research?)
- What was the outcome?

---

6   *Matthew Henry's Commentary.* "Job to Song of Solomon (3 of 6)." Hendrickson Publishers, 1991, p. 779.

You can still maintain an attitude of humility just by stating the facts. The facts speak for themselves. Trying to sell yourself or "praise yourself" by taking all the credit only comes across as self-serving and prideful.

There is a difference between "praising yourself" and communicating facts. Now, if you are saying, "I'm just good at what I do and that's a fact," that is entirely the wrong perspective. That is taking credit instead of recognizing where your skills and abilities come from. What are some things to consider when preparing to be interviewed for a new job?

1. Remember who grants you favor.

God has granted you the skill-set and talents for success. God's sovereignty aligns the circumstances to grant you success or failure in your endeavors. Don't take credit where credit isn't due. Praise Him for this, and remember it in preparing for and during a job interview.

2. Pray for wisdom.

Is this a job that God is leading you to consider? What is your motivation for pursuing this role? Or, if you were contacted directly and asked for interest, is this role a God-honoring one? I have turned down pursuing different roles for a variety of reasons. Sometimes the product or industry was not a God-honoring one, and other times I perceived the work environment would be a challenging place to be. Are you pursuing personal financial gain or status? There is nothing wrong with accepting a role that puts you in a better position financially. However, is this financial gain at a sacrifice to your family or your relationship with God? These are tough questions that you must place before God in prayer.

3. Remember, it's in God's hands.

If you are meant to have this job, God will have already ordained it. He will have prepared you with the experience and skill-set necessary to be successful. He will have already moved in the necessary hearts to make it happen (Proverbs 21:1). There are many positions that I thought were the "perfect fit" for me but God had other plans (Isaiah 55:8-9).

4. Research the company and the position.

How can you best serve an organization? Learn all you can about the company and the expectations of the role. This shows that you have a sincere interest in the company. This is also a great resource to develop a list of questions for the interview. Doing your research gives you an idea of whether the role and company are a good fit for you.

5. Have a good resume.

Resumes should tell a story, not just list education, experience, or past roles. What have you accomplished in those roles that are relevant to the position you are interviewing for? Provide numeric results (e.g., saved the company $2,000 in costs, increased sales by 20 percent, or improved productivity by 12 percent). These tangible results really stand out in a resume and get you noticed.

6. Know the value you bring.

What accomplishments had the biggest impact? What return or value did that bring to the organization you worked for? Be sure you work this into your interview. Be specific. Talk about a time where you were either presented with or uncovered a business-related issue, how you addressed it, and what positive long-term result it delivered.

7. Again, don't try and sell yourself.

Let the results speak for themselves. You do not have to sell results. Don't fall into the trap of self-edification and self-promotion. Most folks can see right through that. Organizations do not want to hire an individual who is only out for their own self-interest. Display a heart to meet the organization's desired needs and how you have successfully served current or previous organizations.

8. Praise God regardless of the outcome.

God has already determined how He can best be glorified. This could manifest in being selected for a new job or *not being selected*. Either way, it is in God's power and control, and we praise Him in either respect. Failure to do so is displaying a lack of trust in God's loving hand in our lives. He loves us dearly and seeks the best for us in the circumstances He ordains.

Interviewing doesn't have to be as nerve-racking as we make it out to be. If we focus on the ways we can best serve the organization in the role, and communicate factual information, then we take the focus off ourselves and seek to honor God in the interview process. If we are not given the role, we trust in God's sovereignty, which helps take the focus off our own bruised ego and pride.

For Further Study

1. Read 2 Corinthians 10:18. Where is our praise to come from? What is the spiritual danger of commending oneself?
2. Read Philippians 2:3-4. How would this apply to being interviewed as described above?

SECTION 3

ENVIRONMENT

Chapter 12

Unethical Behavior in the Workplace

There have been occasions throughout my career when co-workers or even managers have asked me to do something I considered unethical. Most of those times, my first reaction was to quickly refuse, but other times I was extremely uncomfortable and anxious.

The situations that caused me the most discomfort were those where I was concerned that a co-worker would react negatively if I refused, and the rare occasions when a superior was the one making the request. The specific requests ranged from turning a blind eye to improperly logging time, to terminating an employee without following company policy or legal requirements.

The motivation for these kinds of requests can range from simple ignorance to willful intent. In the most extreme cases, there are federal and state laws that support a moral and ethical work environment, but even in federal or state law there is no clear-cut definition that covers every aspect of ethical or unethical behavior. I also acknowledge that it is impossible to address every specific unethical situation you may face, but there are some clear scriptural passages that we can use as a guide.

So, what should you do when you are asked to do something that you consider unethical?

Before we go any further, let's define the term "unethical." How about this: anything contrary to God's moral law is unethical. In other words, God defines ethical and unethical behavior. As Creator, He establishes the standard. Not us. That's important to remember because anytime we are faced with an ethical dilemma, our first response should be to filter it through God's moral law and not our own opinion. Something that offends us personally may not offend God and hence not fall into the definition of unethical conduct. Only when the act or behavior is an offense to God is it to be considered unethical.

Considering that, I thought the most appropriate passage to demonstrate God's moral law is the 10 Commandments. (Exodus 20:1-17) Pause here. Take some time to read this passage. I believe that almost every ethical challenge we face in the workplace can fall into one or more of these commandments, so this is a great place to start. Now, lest you consider this passage outdated, remember Christ's words in Matthew 5:17-19:

> *"Do not think that I have come to abolish the Law or the Prophets; I have not come to abolish them but to fulfill them. For truly, I say to you, until heaven and earth pass away, not an iota, not a dot, will pass from the Law until all is accomplished. Therefore, whoever relaxes one of the least of these commandments and teaches others to do the same will be called least in the kingdom of heaven, but whoever does them and teaches them will be called great in the kingdom of heaven."*

The Law is to be followed perfectly, every time. We can't do that. As Christ tells us in the passage above, He is the only one who fulfills the Law perfectly. We have all broken one or more of these commandments and have been tempted to break several others! But we are still commanded to work heartily at upholding them through the strength and spirit of Christ (Philippians 4:13). And, when we fail (and we will), the only place to turn is to the One who is perfect in every way. Only through our faith in Christ and His perfect life do we have the desire and ability to live righteously and pursue Christlike (and ethical) behavior.

So, in accordance with our personal responsibility to pursue righteousness, let's review some of these commandments in the context of our contemporary work environment. For example, some of us make an idol out of work. We are more consumed with a successful career than our relationship with Christ. On the flip side, some of us try to avoid hard work, and the thought of working more than we want is antithetical to our slothful attitude. Are we honoring our employer, who is the authority that God has placed over us? Are we guarding our relationships at work, so they don't become more personal than they should? Do we work diligently, or do we cheat on timecards and expense reports? Have you taken company supplies home? Have you ever lied to your boss to cover a mistake? Are you envious of a co-worker's position or pay to the point that you believe you are more worthy than they are?

Now, I know that you're probably thinking, *I thought this was about what to do when someone else is being unethical.* We will get there, but Christ first commands us to pull the log out of our own eye before we can accurately confront someone else's sin (Matthew 7:4-5). No one is perfect, and we are not above falling into the same sinful traps we are prepared to confront in others. That is important to remember as we prepare to judge and confront unethical behavior in the workplace.

Another important thing to remember is that each situation and circumstance involving the confrontation of unethical behavior is different. If you are not clear on what direction to take in a certain situation, find a personal contact who understands morality and ethics from a biblical, and even legal, perspective and can look at your situation objectively.

One caveat: I am not addressing the complex issue of blatant illegal and unlawful behavior in the workplace. Dealing with illegal behavior is an extremely sensitive process that only certain qualified individuals in your organization should address. If you become aware of illegal activity in the workplace or someone asks you to do something unlawful, contact your Human Resources or Legal Department immediately. Some companies even have a designated hotline or email address you can contact anonymously if necessary. Do not attempt to confront individuals on your own whom you suspect of illegal or unlawful behavior.

Now, having taken the above into consideration and relying on the strength of our hope in Christ, here are some ways you can exemplify and stand for ethical behavior in the workplace:

1. Live a life beyond reproach.

Read Titus 2:1-10 and 1 Timothy 3:1-13. Though these passages include the qualifications of an Elder and Deacon within the church, they also includes character qualities to which all believers should aspire. If others know that you live a life of utmost character, people are less likely to approach you about doing something unethical.

2. Don't be afraid to take a stand.

Call out unethical behavior by following the principles of Matthew 18:15-18, even in the workplace. When you are asked to perform, or you uncover, a particular action that crosses an ethical line, don't be afraid to call it out. Confidently, but respectfully, confront the individual(s) and state the reason(s) that it is unethical. In some cases, God opens the door to share your faith in the gospel. Be prepared to share Christ if the individual is humbled with your confrontation. But, amazingly, in many cases, the offender reacts in an adversarial or defensive attitude for fear of the consequences of being found out. Don't get into a moral argument when an individual reacts this way. Your confrontation alone will not convict them of their sin. If an individual reacts negatively and the issue is serious enough or there is a habitual pattern of this behavior, you may have to take the next step.

3. If necessary, bring it forward to your superiors.

Still following the Matthew 18:15-18 approach, if this unethical behavior is of a serious enough nature or reveals a pattern of unethical behavior, you have a responsibility to raise the issue with responsible leaders within your organization. No ethical individual wants to work in an unethical organization and no organization who desires to operate ethically wants an unethical reputation. Have specific details and examples. No generalities. A word of caution: Be wise in bringing a questionable issue into the open. You are not the moral conscience of the organization. Only bring issues forward that jeopardize the operation of the business and/ or its reputation.

4. Persevere!

Individuals who stand for godly, moral principles in the workplace always stand on firm ground when the storms come. Don't be tempted to cave into spiritual pressure. It may resolve itself quickly, or it may be a long road with many bumps and twists, and potentially even financial setbacks. But persevere and trust in God, and His desire for you to stand boldly for Him.

5. Be prepared to suffer for your stance.

Sometimes a supervisor or manager makes an unethical or potentially illegal request. Don't sacrifice God's moral principles at the altar of job security. This is admittedly a tough principle. Many people are struggling financially and the thought of sacrificing a job that provides for the welfare of the family to stand for godly principles is a tough pill to swallow. But God always honors your commitment to Him. It may not be in the way you desire or envision it, but know that He is pleased when you stand for, and trust in, His righteousness (1 Peter 4:19). Remember Joseph; he gave up a highly successful position and was even unjustly thrown in jail when he chose to flee an ungodly situation (Genesis 39: 8-12), and what men meant for evil, God meant for good (Genesis 50:19-20; Romans 8:28-29).

6. And, just like Joseph, be prepared to flee from ungodly behavior.

Joseph was prepared spiritually to honor God with his conduct; we are called to be prepared in much the same way. There may be organizations where unethical and even illegal behavior is rampant and there is nowhere to turn. These are the organizations to flee from.

Leaving an organization for this reason is a last resort. Before you make this life-altering decision, be certain that the organization is intentionally ignoring and dishonoring God in their conduct and behavior and not simply offending you personally. Spend significant time in prayer and seek godly counsel with people you trust before making this decision. Failure to do so would lead to a prideful reaction.

Remember, evaluating ethics is not a matter of humanistic reasoning and rationalization. We don't make that determination. God is the ethical standard. We are to stand for Him and be bold in living and proclaiming His standards. Only by confronting and admitting our own failures do we have the credibility to encourage others in godly, ethical behavior. God places us in certain situations to be an example of Christlikeness and to proclaim His gospel. We are called to be witnesses and standard bearers for His truth, not our own. Take courage in this charge.

For Further Study

1. Read Matthew 7:4-5. Are there any ethical situations that you need to confess to God?

2. Read Acts 5:1-11. What was unethical about Ananias and Saphira's conduct?

3. Read John 12:1-6. Discuss Judas' behavior and conduct while a disciple of Jesus.

4. Read John 13:21-30. How did Jesus react to Judas?

Chapter 13

Inappropriate Speech at Work

A major cultural challenge in today's workplace is to live within the world without having it influence the way we live our Christian lives. Many times, I find myself in awkward work conversations that fall into inappropriate jokes or comments. I must admit, avoiding engagement in or reacting to those conversations is difficult. Sometimes the jokes or comments are actually clever and amusing. However, some of the speech is more direct and intentionally hurtful. Cutting sarcasm and crass talk, humorous or not, has no place within the Christian walk.

Our words have impact. They can be used to harm or heal, criticize, or encourage, slander or compliment, attract people to the gospel of Christ or repel people from it. The tongue is to be bridled and controlled. James says,

"If anyone thinks he is religious and does not bridle his tongue but deceives his heart, this person's religion is worthless" (James 1:26).

James makes a powerful correlation. If we are unable or unwilling to control our tongue and speech, our commitment to Christ is worthless! We are to be deliberate with our words, to be slow to speak. A quick tongue, even a quick wit, is to be used cautiously. We are to use our words to encourage and edify to point others to Christ. Paul writes to the Ephesians:

> "But sexual immorality and all impurity or covetousness must not even be named among you, as is proper among saints. Let there be no filthiness nor foolish talk nor crude joking, which are out of place, but instead let there be thanksgiving. For you may be sure of this, that everyone who is sexually immoral or impure, or who is covetous (that is, an idolater), has no inheritance in the kingdom of Christ and God." (Ephesians 5:3-5)

Interestingly, Paul's thoughts flow from immorality, impurity, and greed to the unfit behaviors of filthiness, silly talk, and coarse jesting, as if all the behaviors are related in a spiritual sense. In fact, a heart prone to one group of sins will naturally incline to engage in the others.

Our speech is not to be filthy or silly. Even though we may not actively be engaging in the corresponding behavior, filthy and/or silly speech is making light of the gross sins of immorality against God. It can be argued it is condoning these gross, immoral sins and not edifying God-honoring behavior.

Paul addresses coarse jesting in this scripture as well. This is not an innocent, fun-loving jest between good friends. This is jesting that is intended to "put down" the recipient and make them appear ridiculous using coarse and offensive language. Matthew Henry's commentary on Ephesians 5 states:

". . . obscene and lewd discourse, or more generally, such vain discourse as betrays much folly and indiscretion, and is far from edifying the hearers . . . the context seems to restrain it to such pleasantry of discourse as is filthy and obscene, which he may also design by that corrupt or putrid and rotten, communication that he speaks of . . . those things do not become Christians, and are very unsuitable to their profession and character." [7]

In this passage, Paul not only instructs us to refrain from ungodly speech, but he tells us what should be coming out of our mouths: thankful and grateful speech.

Thankful and grateful speech comes directly from a thankful and grateful heart. When our hearts are aligned with the gospel, then it overflows with gratefulness, for "out of the heart, the mouth speaks" (Matthew 15:18).

Speech starts within our hearts. Actively engaging in or enjoying this type of behavior reveals exactly where our heart is. My loving wife likes to remind me that our first reaction always reveals our heart attitude. We are either seeking to honor Christ or protecting ourselves out of a fear of man.

How does this apply to our work environment? Here are some things to consider:

1. Are you actively engaging in this ungodly talk and behavior?

It's one thing to be an innocent bystander, but another to be actively participating in, or laughing at, ungodly speech. Search

---

7   *Matthew Henry's Commentary.* "Acts to Revelation (6 of 6)." Hendrickson Publishers, 1991, p. 572.

your heart for any hint of enjoying this behavior or even seeking out those who "make you laugh" with coarse jesting. Repent of this and stop seeking opportunities to engage (Matthew 12:33-37).

2. Quietly remove yourself.

If you suddenly find yourself in a situation where the speech becomes harsh, critical, or includes demeaning insults of someone else, quietly remove yourself. Some may feel bold enough to call out the guilty party with the inappropriate talk or behavior. Praise God for this boldness in standing up for Him. Others are not equipped for this.

3. Don't play to the boss.

If you have a supervisor who engages in this behavior, don't fall for the trick of "playing to the boss." If the behavior is not godly, it's not godly, regardless of the individual. I would recommend sitting silently and not responding, reacting, or engaging. Change the subject to a work-related issue. If he or she persists, then calmly excuse yourself and suggest rescheduling the meeting. "You obviously have other things on your mind, perhaps another time would be better to discuss this issue. I will schedule some time on your calendar."

4. Actively direct the speech toward positive encouragement.

If someone is speaking inappropriately about (or to) a fellow co-worker, state a positive attribute or characteristic of the individual (e.g., "I have found that John responds very quickly to anything I need from him," or, "Did you know that Mary volunteers at the local hospital's maternity ward on the weekends?") In most cases, this stops or slows the discussion. However, other times it only creates a need for the individual to justify their attacks. Don't respond or engage, just restate your positive experiences with the person.

5. Don't be a complainer!

Are you a complainer at your workplace or are you one who is thankful for the job God has given you? It is not uncommon for co-workers to sit in the break room over lunch and complain about work situations or superiors. Even though this would technically not qualify as "filthy" speech, it still qualifies as ungodly speech and must be controlled and replaced with appropriate, temperate speech.

6. Stick to the facts.

Don't engage in gossip or unsubstantiated rumors. Scripture is clear about these issues (Proverbs 20:19; Romans 1:29; 2 Corinthians 12:20).

7. Encourage others.

Intentionally find ways to encourage others with your words. There are individuals in every organization that work very diligently to serve you and their fellow employees. Intentionally recognize this trait and sincerely and graciously thank them for it. You will be surprised how rarely this is done. You will be blessed to hear and see their reaction. We are called to encourage one another (1 Thessalonians 5:11; Hebrews 3:13).

8. Caution!

If you hear any reference to something that could be illegal, threatening, or abusive, you have an obligation to report it to your manager or human resources. Failure to do so may be perceived as complying with or condoning this type of behavior. Be wise in this. It must not be a trivial complaint but one that a reasonable person would consider as crossing a line.

James reminds us that "from the same mouth come blessing and cursing. My brothers, these things ought not to be so" (James 3:10). Our speech should always be a blessing by pointing others to Christ either by an encouragement or an admonishment, nothing else. Guard your heart first by filling it full of the truth of Scripture and reminding ourselves of how the gospel of Christ has saved us from the sinful desire to use our tongues for anything else.

For Further Study

1. Read Matthew 12: 33-37. Do our words matter to God? How?
2. Read Matthew 23:27-28. How does this relate to ungodly speech?
3. Read Proverbs 20:19, Romans 1:29, and 2 Corinthians 12:20. What stands out to you in each of these passages?
4. Read 1 Thessalonians 5:11 and Hebrews 3:13. What should be the focus of our speech?
5. Recall a time where the sting of ungodly speech affected you directly. Why did it hurt?
6. What is the godly reaction? Are you convicted by your own engagement in this behavior?
7. Is there anyone that needs your encouragement? How and when will you display this?

Chapter 14

Handling Sexual Harassment Situations

S exual harassment situations and complaints in the workplace are especially serious and usually very complex.
Throughout my Human Resources career, I have dealt with
and investigated such issues as a plant manager who had an inti-
mate relationship with an hourly employee, a married supervisor
who pursued a homosexual relationship with his subordinate, a
manager who allegedly exposed himself to a female co-worker, and
many complaints of sexually explicit comments and behavior.

What I learned throughout my career is that every situation is
unique due to the variety of people, the varying circumstances, the
emotional reactions of the involved parties, and the expected outcomes. No two situations of sexual harassment are ever the same
and must be investigated and handled differently. My goal in this
chapter is to give you guidance on your initial reaction, the subsequent steps, and how to deal with this from a biblical perspective.
Before we talk about that, let's go through a quick summary definition of harassment and discrimination from a legal standpoint.

From a legal standpoint, complaints of sexual harassment must be responded to immediately, although resolution through the investigative process takes some time. I want to tell you up front that this article is not meant to provide legal advice or counsel. It is imperative that you seek out your Legal and/or HR department immediately when you become aware of a sexual harassment complaint.

Sexual harassment is a form of sex discrimination that violates Title VII of the Civil Rights Act of 1964. Title VII applies to employers with 15 or more employees, including state and local governments.

Unwelcome sexual advances, requests for sexual favors, and other verbal or physical conduct of a sexual nature constitute sexual harassment when this conduct explicitly or implicitly affects an individual's employment, unreasonably interferes with an individual's work performance, or creates an intimidating, hostile, or offensive work environment.

Sexual harassment can occur in a variety of circumstances, including but not limited to the following:

- The victim as well as the harasser may be a woman or a man. The victim does not have to be of the opposite sex.
- The harasser can be the victim's supervisor, an agent of the employer, a supervisor in another area, a co-worker, or a non-employee.
- The victim does not have to be the person harassed but could be anyone affected by the offensive conduct.
- Unlawful sexual harassment may occur without economic injury to or discharge of the victim.
- The harasser's conduct must be unwelcome.

Although it is helpful for the victim to inform the harasser directly that the conduct is unwelcome and must stop, it is not a legal requirement. The victim may use any employer complaint or grievance process available to them, either verbal or written.

When investigating allegations of sexual harassment, the whole record is considered: the circumstances, such as the nature of the sexual advances, and the context in which the alleged incidents occurred. A determination on the allegations is made from the facts on a case-by-case basis.

Prevention is the best tool to eliminate sexual harassment in the workplace. Employers are encouraged to take steps necessary to prevent sexual harassment from occurring. They should clearly communicate to employees that sexual harassment will not be tolerated. They can do so by providing sexual harassment training to their employees and by establishing an effective complaint or grievance process and taking immediate and appropriate action when an employee complains.

It is also unlawful to retaliate against an individual for opposing employment practices that discriminate based on sex or for filing a discrimination charge, testifying, or participating in any way in an investigation, proceeding, or litigation under Title VII.

That was a very quick overview of the legal definition and requirements of a sexual harassment complaint.

The most biblical advice I can give regarding this situation is found in Proverbs:

"The one who states his case first seems right, until the other comes and examines him." (Proverbs 18:17)

There is profound wisdom in this simple proverb:

1. An individual is pleading a case as to a judge or one in authority.

People in positions of authority wield power in the workplace. Jobs are a source of income and provision for employees. Victims of sexual harassment reach out to those in power to be protected against immoral behavior and are truly seeking help and guidance. God has established rulers and authorities as a means of establishing a moral authority in cases such as these. Unfortunately, some of those in authority abuse their positions and undermine God's established structures—some as perpetrators, and others by "turning a blind eye" to this behavior by not believing the accusers or refusing to address the issues out of fear or ignorance.

2. There are two sides to every story.

We are generally quick to believe the first side of any story we hear. In some respects, we must react to the initial claim as if it were 100 percent true, however we must not underreact, or overreact. Whenever someone brings a serious issue forward, it sounds extremely ominous. The more ominous it sounds, the more anxious we get. We feel the need to address and take corrective action immediately against the accused party. I have found many times that my first reaction to an issue is usually emotional and reactive based on limited information. This is exactly what false accusers are counting on. We must resist this reaction. Although the first to plead his case "seems right," the facts must substantiate the claim. Truthful accusers are not afraid of scrutiny and welcome an investigation of the facts to corroborate their claims. They want the truth to come out and will assist in every way they can if they feel protected. For others, especially those who have been participating in or encouraging inappropriate behavior, getting their story out before the other party is a form of protection and survival by laying blame on others before they themselves are accused.

3. Those in authority must investigate and listen to all sides of a story before a judgment is made.
One in authority has a responsibility to reserve judgment until every detail is examined. This is important information to communicate to all involved parties. Some expect immediate resolution based on their traumatic experience and subsequent demands. Establishing the expectation up front, while respecting the integrity of the investigative process, is important. However, regular updates to impacted parties are important and necessary.

We will now deal with this issue from four different perspectives:
1. The Victim
2. The Accused
3. The Manager
4. The Witness

The Victim.
Everyone has the right to work in an environment free from harassment and abuse of any kind. If you believe that any of the above Title VII guidelines have been violated, you have the right and the *responsibility* to report any violation of these rights. Every organization has the legal obligation to address these issues *immediately* out of protection for their employees. Any delay only emboldens the perpetrator and increases the possibility of this kind of behavior spreading throughout the culture. If you have any doubts, questions, or fears, bring them forward to your

manager or your Human Resources Department. Perpetrators are counting on victims not reporting this behavior out of fear.

There is also a legal obligation of protection against retaliation when this type of behavior is reported. Many organizations now have an anonymous employee hotline. However, be sure that what you are reporting falls under the legal definition of harassment and not unprofessional behavior. You want to be sure that the appropriate issue is being addressed and not discounted because of terminology.

If you have an immediate fear for your safety, clearly state this to your manager or Human Resources. Organizational leadership has an obligation to protect their employees to the best of their ability in these cases. If you believe that your physical well-being is in immediate danger, alert the authorities. You also have the right to request a leave of absence or a transfer to another department/location. Although the company is not obligated to comply, it may be taken under consideration if you believe it is in your best interests or safety.

Throughout the investigative process, from your initial report going forward, state the facts clearly and succinctly. This will aid in the investigation. Every detail is important. Include dates, times, and circumstances of every event. Provide names of witnesses to any event or conversation (if any). It's okay to provide second-hand knowledge of other events if another victim relays them to you. This information will obviously need to be verified; however, it could aid in the investigation, especially if it corroborates your experience. Avoid providing third-hand knowledge of events unrelated to you and which does not relate specifically to your own experience. This only confuses the facts of the investigation.

Emotions will be difficult to manage during this process, especially if harassment has been occurring for any length of time. If you are not provided regular updates to the investigation or have not been given a time when you should receive any updates or conclusion, you should request one. Be patient. Complex investigations take time to prove. It's not that your statement is not believed, but it must be proven to be factual if any action is to be taken. Investigators are also not required to provide a hasty resolution or acquiesce to your demands (e.g., termination or transfer). The conclusions and outcome will be based on the results of an investigation.

The Accused.

It is critical that you do not act on your initial emotions. This could have a negative impact to you and the investigation. When presented with the accusation, acknowledge your reaction, but pause before you respond. State your response clearly and concisely. If the accusation is untrue or lacks a factual basis, offer a firm denial, and provide any evidence or witnesses that can attest to your statement. Respectfully answer direct questions regarding the events of the accusation. Respond only to the facts of the accusation as they have been presented, not your emotional reaction to them. Anything else could confuse the situation.

If, unfortunately, the accusations are true, don't lie. Admit your fault or involvement. Even if the work environment is such that the inappropriate behavior has become commonplace, that doesn't make it right. You were wrong to participate, but it also doesn't excuse anyone's behavior. If you have been a witness to any illegal or inappropriate behavior, you have a responsibility to state evidence of that. You also have a right to be kept apprised of the investigation's progress. Ask for a follow-up meeting if one has not been offered. Above all, it is imperative that you are completely accurate of the facts, even if you bear some responsibility. I need not remind you of your obligation to God to be truthful.

The Manager.

You will most likely be the one who receives the first allegation of wrongdoing. Your initial reaction is crucial. Many managers make the mistake of discounting the accusations based on their own preconceived notions. That is a costly legal mistake. If any perceived sexual harassment is reported, you now have a legal obligation to investigate. Failure to do so puts you and the company at risk. Depending on the circumstance, you could be held personally liable as well. Your job at this point is to get as many facts as possible.

Ask clarifying questions: Who? What? When? Where? If the employee doesn't feel safe, offer to send the employee home. Don't make a determination based on the initial information and don't offer one. Promise that the company will investigate the accusations to the best of their ability. Immediately notify your Human Resources and Legal Departments.

You need to be responsive and cautious. I have had many individuals file a complaint of harassment on another individual to cover up a sin of their own. Either they were initially engaging and participating, and another party went too far, or they began to fear for their own job because of this participation and laid the blame on the other party before it came out. Others file a complaint on a manager or supervisor after they are held accountable to performing their job duties. I have received many reports of harassment or discrimination where the individual's sole purpose was an attempt to distract the organization from the real issue of poor performance or inappropriate behavior on the part of the accuser. This only discredits real acts of sexual harassment and discrimination that need to be addressed.

Bottom line, be timely and responsive to the complaint, listen, gather facts, do not offer any solutions, and immediately notify your legal team and Human Resources.

The Witness.

A witness to sexually harassing or hostile behavior also has a responsibility—not only a biblical one (Psalm 94:14-16), but a legal one. Let's say for example, that a situation escalates to the point where the complaint is brought to legal authorities and charges are filed. If you are witness to behavior or events that should have been reported, then you can be held personally liable for the neglect to report.

Although we should not confront or engage the instigator of the behavior unless it becomes an issue of physical safety, we simply do not have the option to "not get involved" if we witness harassing or hostile behavior. But again, I would exercise caution. Be sure that the behavior qualifies as harassing or hostile per the above Title VII criteria. Some behavior, although inappropriate, would be defined as unprofessional but not illegal. Speak one-on-one with your manager or supervisor first if the behavior is of concern to you. If your organization has an anonymous way to report this type of behavior (hotline or email), this is an option for you as well. Obviously keep a record of who you reported this to (date and time). This protects you in case of escalation. If the behavior is a pattern, make sure that you provide specifics in your report as well as additional witnesses. Only report the facts of what you heard or observed as well as the names of other witnesses. Don't make any assumptions. Do not discuss the events with your co-workers because this could unintentionally escalate the situation, and if the instigator learns that other people are talking about him or her, you could become a target yourself.

Again, these situations are extremely complex and will require the assistance of senior leaders within your organization, primarily your legal team and your Human Resources professionals. Do not take these issues too lightly, but ensure that you are taking the appropriate steps to protect yourself and your co-workers by understanding and interpreting your biblical and legal responsibilities appropriately.

For Further Study

1. Read 1 Kings 3:16-28. How did Solomon apply Proverbs 18:17 (which he wrote) to control his initial reactions and discern the truth?

2. Read Romans 3:21-26. If God is just, and the ultimate authority and judge, how is He also the justifier?

Chapter 15

Workplace Diversity

After this I looked, and behold, a great multitude that no one could number, from every nation, from all tribes and peoples and languages, standing before the throne and before the Lamb, clothed in white robes, with palm branches in their hands, and crying out with a loud voice, "Salvation belongs to our God who sits on the throne, and to the Lamb!" (Revelation 7:9-10)

How I long for this day! A day where the worship of Christ has unified all believers into one multitude, one place, and one voice. All focus is centered on the Lamb of God. No more sin. No more sorrow. No more distractions from the joyful worship and glory of Christ. A glorious and joyful day!

This passage is a beautiful picture and reminder that God is the author and creator of diverse nations and cultures, evident by the fact that this beauty will extend into eternity! When we focus on this truth, we begin to realize that our diversity is a glorious display of Creator God. The beauty of God's perspective on diversity is that when we, as believers, demonstrate unity within and amongst one another, even amidst our varied ethnic, gender, generational, and cultural backgrounds, through the common bond of the gospel, we glorify God and His unifying purpose. The future day described in this passage is a culmination of God's gracious hand extended to all people.

But this day is still yet to come.

We live in a deeply depraved and sinful world. One that is not unified. Oppression, racial bigotry, child trafficking, physical and sexual abuse, and more are all alive and well. But we cannot give up. We are to fight fervently against these injustices alongside our Christian brothers and sisters. We are to love and honor all people as uniquely created by God. However, as Christians, we must realistically recognize that all our human efforts and initiatives will only go so far. They will never truly eliminate these injustices.

Several corporations have brought the effort of fighting human injustices into the workplace through the concept of workplace diversity. This concept has become a core principle of corporate culture, marketing, and politics. Corporations have adopted all-inclusive diversity policies to appease every identifiable culture, race, and gender (biological and otherwise). This effort to appease everyone has ultimately proven to be elusive because the number of designated subsets and representations continues to increase. It has become difficult to keep track. People can identify with literally dozens of sub-cultures. Corporations design internal and external marketing initiatives to win over potential customers, clients, and even employees from these infinitely increasing sub-cultures.

Organizational diversity programs at their core are well-meaning and, at times necessary to correct an organization's lack of focus in this area. For example, if an organization's leadership is primarily of one race or gender, then appropriate initiatives should be implemented to train, educate, and develop all people for success within the organization regardless of ethnicity, race, or gender. But, any program that focuses simply on improving diversity representation metrics without preparation creates a false premise that physical differences are the most valuable aspect of diversity rather than the idea that God's gifting and life experiences create the value. This false premise defeats the very purpose, and the program will not succeed.

One event in particular opened my eyes to this failure. I was a Regional HR Lead for a publicly held company and was giving a corporate presentation that included diversity metrics for the region. I reported our progress to date. A short while later, one of the regional leaders stood up to make his own presentation. He started out by saying, "I just want to say a few words about diversity. I am a black man, and I don't want anyone promoting or hiring me for my diversity. I want to be promoted because I'm good at my job!" I was stunned. I suddenly realized that the organization was focusing strictly on diversity metrics and not the people. This statistical focus was detrimental and insulting to the very people groups that it was supposedly supporting.

I further realized that the most prevalent corporate solution to the issue of workplace diversity was falsely placing hope in the efforts of celebrating human differences above the unifying call of Christ. While the concept of respect for all people is a valid one and worthy of pursuit, blindly separating people into self-proclaimed subsets is not a biblical one. However, this perspective is not new. The people of Galatia had this very problem. Paul tells us in Galatians:

"For in Christ Jesus you are all sons of God, through faith. For as many of you as were baptized into Christ have put on Christ. There is neither Jew nor Greek, there is neither slave nor free, there is no

male and female, for you are all one in Christ Jesus. And if you are Christ's, then you are Abraham's offspring, heirs according to promise." (Galatians 3:26-29)

The Galatians were dividing themselves based on ethnic identities rather than understanding that Christ had grafted all believers into His "chosen race." Those of us in Christ are His brothers and sisters. We are fellow heirs with Him in God's eternal plan. At the cross, Christ obliterated all man-centered identities.

In other words, believers are unified in Christ alone. We find our identity in what He did on the cross for us—not in worldly labels. If we are to celebrate, we are to rejoice that we have been adopted into God's loving family. We also, being one in Him, display the spiritual outpouring of love and care for our brothers and sisters in Christ and a grieving heart for lost souls. We are called to a greater love than the world demands: to display the love of Christ. He alone is the unifier of all races and cultures. No corporate diversity initiative or goal can accomplish that.

Another polarizing issue closely related to diversity is the gender pronoun debate. Individuals are claiming the right to self-identify their gender and how they wish to be referred. The traditional gender pronouns of *he* and *she* are being rejected for more self-expressive terms. This could vary based on the individual's preferences rather than their actual biological anatomy. Individuals might identify as male or female based strictly on their own self-identity. Others might consider themselves "gender fluid," which means that they could identify as male one day, female another, or genderless the next. Gender fluid individuals might identify as equally male and female at any given time.

Some people completely reject the concept of gender. They indicate that they cannot, or will not, identify with any current or traditional classification of gender. They consider themselves unique from every individual with a unique identity. They consider themselves uncategorized by any gender labels and have created their own separate classification with their own nomenclature.

As you can see, this issue is a moving target and supporters cannot maintain any long-term, consistent perspective. People seek individuality in their gender self-identification with no possible predictability. Everyone else is left in a state of confusion coupled with the fear of offending the individual at any given moment.

People have only a few options when confronted with this issue:

1. Address the individual with their preferred pronoun.

Some believers, in choosing this option, refer to Paul's comments in 1 Corinthians 8 or Romans 14:13-23 as it pertains to causing another brother to stumble in their spiritual walk. However, these passages refer to the freedom we have in Christ of believers receiving food sacrificed to idols, which Jewish law prohibited. Paul's assertion is that it does not matter that a particular food had been previously sacrificed to idols. It does not impact our position in Christ. However, if eating the food previously sacrificed to idols causes another to stumble, affirming that idols must be "okay," then we are to refrain from eating. In applying this to the gender pronoun debate, some argue that acquiescing to an individual's preferences on a temporary basis leaves the door open to further gospel discussion. But then, predictability becomes an issue. How do you refer to someone at any given moment? A counterargument can be made that it gives credence and validity to the preference and closes the door to any further discussion, in effect, causing others to stumble.

2. Use gender-neutral pronouns.

Indicate that you will refer to everyone (or perhaps the individual) as "this person or that person," or, "they or them." If an individual persists, you may say something to the effect, "I respect your rights, and hopefully you can respect my deeply held religious beliefs. I believe that this compromise can achieve both objectives." If used unilaterally and consistency, this usually avoids any charges of discrimination. Conforming to this change in terminology takes practice. Be prepared for multiple failures.

3. Take a stand.

There have been multiple lawsuits filed (domestically and internationally) in the gender pronoun debate, citing violations of free speech and/or religious freedom. Individuals adamantly refuse to capitulate to an individual's self-proclaimed gender. This takes sacrifice at a very individual and personal level. Individuals have been fired, ridiculed, and their reputations ruined. But that is the risk some people feel called by God to bear in the face of direct opposition to God's created order.

This issue is admittedly a difficult one. Believers must honor God in every aspect of life and stand for His principles. If any of our words or actions gives validity to an ungodly and secular perspective, then we dishonor God. In the case of the gender pronoun debate, validating an individual's separation from God's sovereignty in His intended creation design is actually a stumbling block to our witness of the gospel. I encourage you to give this issue some serious thought and prayer and not simply "go with the flow" of secular perspectives.

All these efforts have resulted in more division, not less. The Enemy has always used our human efforts and reasoning against us. He seeks to divide rather than unify. It can be argued that all our human efforts to unify people tend to have the reverse effect. It places us into ever-expanding people groups that differentiate from each other rather than bring us together. It negates the unifying life and death of Jesus Christ. However, celebrating these God-ordained differences in a biblical way has the unifying effect the world so desperately seeks.

So, how can we deal with workplace diversity in a biblical way? Here are some ideas:

1. Don't fear our God-ordained differences. Celebrate them!

Recognize and celebrate our differences from God's perspective. He created us male and female with beautifully varying ethnic groups and cultures. There are many different cultures and peoples to celebrate and enjoy in this world. We can learn much from these experiences. Don't fall into the trap of fearing people or attacking cultural ideas that are different than your own. This only leads to more isolation of each other. If the cultural differences are not in conflict with God, embrace them. All people groups are God's created people. Enjoy them as such.

2. Consider other options.

Organizations create multiple and never-ending diversity councils to celebrate every identifiable people group. This leads to competition between the groups. Consider creating a singular diversity council that celebrates all diversity efforts rather than having varying councils compete for funding and recognition. Alternatively, unify the organization around community service or specific charitable and social causes.

3. Remember that spiritual gifts should unite, not divide.

God has ordained us with spiritual gifts, uniquely granted to each individual to further His Kingdom—some to teach, some with the gift of hospitality, some with the gift of evangelism, and many others. But these spiritual gifts should not divide us, as Paul warns in 1 Corinthians 12.

4. Respect authority without compromise.

Many Christians work in organizations that require a certain perspective of diversity that might conflict with biblical principles. You might be requested as part of your job to support these diversity efforts. Jesus says to "render to Caesar what is Caesar's and to God what is God's" (Mark 12:17). If you need this employment to support your family for the foreseeable future and you choose to remain, then you must be prepared to submit to the organization without compromising God's truth (1 Peter 2:16). As in the gender-pronoun debate mentioned earlier, you might offer the compromise of gender-neutral language as a reference to all individuals. Remaining under secular authority in these issues is admittedly a fine line and one that might require you to take a stand at some point (Daniel 3:16-18, 6:10-15). But we are called to live and treat *all* people in a Christ-honoring way, *regardless* of the organization's definition of diversity. Point others to the freedom of the gospel. As Peter challenges us: "Honor everyone. Love the brotherhood. Fear God. Honor the emperor" (1 Peter 2:13-20). The gospel of Christ is primary.

5. Remember we are one in Christ.

We are joint heirs in Christ regardless of physical characteristics (Romans 8:16-18; Ephesians 2:11-22, 3:5-7). Recognize your fellow brothers and sisters in Christ. Look past the worldly defined categories.

6. Don't over-generalize or stereotype.

In your effort to correct legitimate injustices, guard yourself that you don't fall into the trap of making presuppositions, generalizations, or decisions based on culture, race, or gender. In other words, don't automatically assume that your way is the best way to correct the issue. Ask questions. Listen and learn. What is it like to walk in their shoes? What is it like to be them? What are they dealing with or have dealt with? What do they think is the right course of action? Then have a discussion. Stay focused on the main goal of proclaiming the gospel and being a godly witness and example (Acts 10:34-35).

7. Remain humble.

Even as you are exposed to varying races and cultures, remember that no race or culture has worldly superiority over another (Philippians 2:3-4).

8. Remember the gospel is proclaimed to all peoples.

Remember that the gospel is proclaimed to "both Jew and Gentile"—that means all ethnicities (Galatians 3:26-29). A prayer in the *Book of Common Order of the Church of Scotland* encourages us to keep Christ and His message at the forefront of every ethnic relationship:

> *God and Father of all,*
> *in your love*
> *you made all the nations of the world*
> *to be a family,*

and your Son taught us to love one another.
Yet our world is riven apart
with prejudice, arrogance, and pride.
Help the different races
to love and understand one another better.
Increase among us sympathy,
tolerance, and goodwill,
that we may learn to appreciate the gifts
that other races bring to us,
and to see in all people
our brothers and sisters for whom Christ died.
Save us from jealousy, hatred, and fear,
and help us to live together
as members of one family at home in the world,
sons and daughters of one Father
who live in the liberty of the children of God;
through Jesus Christ our Lord. Amen.[8]

We would do well to remember that the gospel of Christ is the only successful unifying force in the world. There is no law or corporate policy that can accomplish what Christ has done on the cross for all believers, regardless of our diversity. Our hope is in Christ alone, not in any of our human efforts. To quote missionary J.D. Crowley, "The gospel drives a cross-shaped dagger into the heart of racism."

Through our diligent efforts, we will win some battles and even have some limited successes, but these victories will never eliminate the sinful root issues of the heart. Human victories will never replace Christ's victorious work on the cross. Injustices will

8   *Book of Common Order of the Church of Scotland*

remain until Christ returns and we are standing before the throne of God. Darrell Johnson notes:

> "The new Israel of God is made up of Jew and Gentiles–Jews and Arabs and Kenyans and Norwegians and Brazilians and Japanese. Multi-cultural, multi-lingual, multi-racial, trans-national. They are all there with the King; ready to sing a new song." [9]

This is our future hope and peace. There will be no more hatred or oppression. We who are in Christ will be singing a new song of worship. We will be in harmony with one another for all eternity. The King of Glory will welcome His people home!

For Further Study

1. Read Colossians 3:9-17. How are we to treat our fellow believers in Christ, regardless of ethnicity?

2. Read Acts 10:34-48. How did God address the Jewish concept of religious superiority and oppression?

3. In what ways have you seen God used as a justification for worldly agendas?

4. Read Deuteronomy 7:7-11. Why did God choose to initially reveal Himself to the Jewish people throughout Bible history?

5. Read Ephesians 6:12. Define our common enemy and identify our resources in this spiritual battle. Does Satan want to divide or unify us? What are some ways he would do that?

---

9   Johnson, D. 2004. *Discipleship on the Edge.* Vancouver, British Columbia: Regent College Publishing, pg. 270.

6. Read 1 Peter 2:13-20. How does this apply to diversity initia-
    tives that don't align with your biblical understanding?
7. Read Ephesians 2:11-22. How did God reconcile the barrier
    between Jew and Gentile?
8. Read 1 Corinthians 1:18-31. What worldly wisdom is Paul
    referring to? How does this apply to your efforts to fight
    injustices?
9. Read John 17:10-11. Relate this to God's unifying desire for
    all people.

Chapter 16

Sharing Our Faith in the Workplace

Expressing our faith publicly is becoming more challenging during this current age, but the workplace itself is not the primary cause of the challenges. It's important to recognize that the workplace is primarily a business that is responding to, and reflective of, the wants and needs of a particular market audience, which is our current secular culture.

The current culture in which we live is becoming increasingly secular and less interested in spiritual things. Businesses react to the marketplace and customer demographics. The attraction of our culture through entertainment, technology, and worldly success is far more appealing to secular people than seeking to understand or submit to any spiritual authority. This has led to a range of reactions to the Christian faith from indifferent tolerance to all-out attacks. Workplace Christians are often tempted to hide their faith out of fear of retaliation or even to protect their job security.

Persecution has been part of the Christian life since the days of the early Church. However, many of us have been protected by the general acceptance of Christianity as part of our culture. That is no longer the case. Religious persecution has come in the form of lawsuits, ridicule, accusations of hypocrisy, and in some cases, violence, and death. In most areas of the world, Christianity is not widely accepted or is becoming increasingly minimized. As a culture becomes less and less accepting of God, it becomes more and more adversarial to Him and His people.

The workplace has become secularized to the point that all faiths are to be celebrated in the name of diversity and inclusion, with no regard for the pursuit of truth. All employees are encouraged to bring their "whole self" to work, including whatever faith or belief or lifestyle that makes you "happy." Christianity is diametrically opposed to the worship of self as a way of life.

Yet, we are commanded to bring the gospel to a hurting and sinful world. How can we do that in an environment that is apathetic, and even hostile, to recognizing or submitting to a creator God? How can we protect ourselves against any threats or violence because of simply being a Christian? How do we honor Christ and keep our livelihood?

God is aware of the world's lack of acceptance of Him. He warns us of this attitude often. Consider the words of Christ in Matthew 10:16-20:

> *"Behold, I am sending you out as sheep in the midst of wolves, so be wise as serpents and innocent as doves. Beware of men, for they will deliver you over to courts and flog you in their synagogues, and you will be dragged before governors and kings for my sake, to bear witness before them and the Gentiles. When they deliver you over, do not be anxious how you are to speak or what you are to say, for what you are to say will be given to you in that hour. For it is not you who speak, but the Spirit of your Father speaking through you."*

Christ goes on in this same chapter of Matthew to tell us the proper place of fear and to trust in God's omniscience and power:

> *"And do not fear those who kill the body but cannot kill the soul. Rather fear him who can destroy both soul and body in hell. Are not two sparrows sold for a penny? And not one of them will fall to the ground apart from your Father. But even the hairs of your head are all numbered. Fear not, therefore; you are of more value than many sparrows. So everyone who acknowledges me before men, I also will acknowledge before my Father who is in heaven, but whoever denies me before men, I also will deny before my Father who is in heaven." (Matthew 10:28-33)*

Obedience to proclaim the gospel of Christ to a hostile world will never be comfortable. But, this passage is referring to more than simply being uncomfortable: Christians faced risks to their physical lives. We forget that following Christ is not designed to be comfortable, or even safe. However, Christ does provide some guidance and wisdom in the face of this persecution.

Matthew Henry comments on "being wise as serpents" in this way:

> "The disciples of Christ are hated and persecuted as serpents, and their ruin is sought, and therefore they need the serpent's wisdom. It is the will of Christ that his people and ministers, being so much exposed to troubles in this world, as they usually are, should not needlessly expose themselves, but use all fair and lawful means for their own preservation. Christ gave us an

example of this wisdom (with) the many escapes He made out of the hands of His enemies, till His hour was come." [10]

There is a wisdom and prudence in living our lives in the face of potential persecution. It's not to "test" God's faithfulness of our obedience to share the gospel or expect deliverance from our enemies when we take actions outside of God's guidance. Living faithfully is a humble reliance on God's Holy Spirit at the proper time. It is being bold in the words we are given rather than expressing the false confidence of our own knowledge. It's not putting ourselves in situations where we are outside of God's obedience. It's having the prudent wisdom to know when we are at risk of doing that.

So, given the command to be bold for Christ and trusting in wisdom, what does that look like in the workplace? We can share the precepts of God and His goodness in many ways without being accused of proselytizing or violating workplace policies and suffering needless consequences. These include:

1. Live a life above reproach.

Read Titus 2:1-10 and 1 Timothy 3:1-13, which encourage us to live our Christian lives in obedience to Him—every day, all day. People will notice that you are different. That you don't engage in crude jokes or criticism of others. That you do not lie, cheat, and steal to better your life or get ahead in the workplace. That you are faithful to and enjoy your spouse. That you consider others before yourself. That you honor God in every aspect of your life.

---

10   *Matthew Henry's Commentary.* "Matthew to John (5 of 6)." Hendrickson Publishers, pg. 113.

A changed heart and life are a tremendous witness to the gospel of Christ.

2. Apply biblical principles to workplace situations.

Living out biblical principles is the most impactful and practical thing you can do in the workplace. A key part of my Human Resources role was applying, and coaching others to apply, biblical principles. I think you will find that most workplace policies are unknowingly designed to enforce biblical principles.

3. Offer to pray.

Most people going through a tough time in life welcome the prayers. Ask what you can pray for specifically and commit to follow through. This is a spiritually uplifting moment for everyone. If you have the opportunity to pray with or for someone at your workplace, follow up with them appropriately. Listening, remembering, and telling them how you specifically prayed for them communicates love in a powerful way.

4. Ask questions.

Express genuine interest in your co-workers' personal lives when appropriate. Maybe they have a family member who is a believer. This is a good discussion point to highlight what it means to be a Christian. If they or a family member are facing a life-threatening illness or medical situation, ask them what gets them through that. You may have the opportunity to share your own experience.

5. Acknowledge God in your own life.

Express gratitude to God for the blessings in your life. "God has certainly given us a beautiful day, hasn't He?" Direct praise to

God for any positive traits you have or compliments you receive rather than accepting all the glory. You can certainly overdo this and sound disingenuous or pretentious, but in the appropriate setting and audience, it points people to the goodness of God and His graciousness to all.

6. Share your own life.

If someone asks you what you did this weekend or what you did on vacation, they have opened a door for you. Offer that up. What did your pastor preach on this Sunday that spoke to you? Just share your life.

7. Be prepared for questions.

If you are a known Christian, don't be blindsided by a surprise attack. "What do you think about abortion? Or homosexuality?" Be prepared to state your position using the authority of Scripture and not your own opinion, which leaves you open to further personal attack. "Well, Scripture tells us that…," or, "I need to get back to you on that." This is acknowledging the truth of God as the ultimate authority and not man's opinions. Don't be afraid to say that you will research that and follow up. This avoids any opinion-centered arguments.

8. Don't expect miracles.

Just because you are faithful to share your faith, the workplace is primarily filled with unbelievers. Unbelievers will continue to act like unbelievers until God has opened their eyes and they accept the gift of salvation and even then, they might not have the spiritual maturity to change certain behaviors until long after. Don't be surprised that individuals are not receptive or open to your faith. Jesus wasn't surprised at the behavior of those who rejected Him. He didn't expect everyone to immediately accept the message of the gospel (Matthew 10:14). However, this does not alleviate our responsibility to be faithful in sharing God's gracious mercy. We are to be lights in the darkness of the world. Keep shining, regardless of the response.

9. Trust in Christ.

This is the hard part. God is sovereign; He is omniscient; He is all-powerful. But, persecution still exists for His followers. He is telling us that He has this world well in hand, even though it may seem to be out of His control. He is calling us to trust that He will provide the words and strength at the proper time, not before. He encourages us to remember that, and not forsake Him in the face of persecution.

There may be times when standing for God in the workplace in the face of severe consequences might be required of you, where refusing to lie or falsify documents could cost you dearly, but that is in God's timing, not ours. Knowing the difference takes a complete reliance on God.

The workplace is a minefield of challenges, but it is also an opportunity to witness for the gospel of Christ. Stay faithful to the redemption you have been given and pray for appropriate opportunities to live and share your faith. God will provide those opportunities along with the strength and words to glorify Himself. He is forever faithful to that promise.

For Further Study

1. Read Chapter 11 of Hebrews. What examples are there of those that have walked by faith?

2. According to Hebrews 11, did walking by faith guarantee an easy life?

3. Do you ever believe that you have tried to force the gospel on an individual at one time or another? Or have you ever observed this happening with someone else? What was the outcome?

4. Has there ever been a time that God blessed you with an unexpected opportunity to talk about your faith? What happened?

5. What are some other ways you can live out or share your faith in your workplace?

SECTION 4

SELF-DOUBT

Chapter 17

Passed Up for a Promotion

Having someone else selected for a job or position that we desire is a very personal issue. We sincerely believe that we have the skill-set, experience, and talent to do the role and we desire to advance to higher levels of status and income to provide a better life for our families. But for reasons either known or unknown to us, sometimes we are not selected. As a result, we can become angry, critical of our leader's judgment, depressed, or even fearful of not meeting retirement goals. Although this is naturally a huge disappointment, we cannot allow sin to control our reaction. When we do, we are displaying a lack of trust in God's sovereignty.

Let's take a step back for a moment and consider our motivations for even pursing a position of higher status. Do we have a pure motivation? Or, deep down, is it really a selfish motivation? Is this promotion something that we desire so deeply that we are willing to sin to get it, or conversely, sin when we don't get it?

The disciples weren't immune to this earthly pursuit. They argued and jockeyed with each other for positional status and greatness in the Kingdom of God. One example of this is in the book of Mark:

> *"And they came to Capernaum. And when he was in the house he asked them, 'What were you discussing on the way?' But they kept silent, for on the way they had argued with one another about who was the greatest." (Mark 9: 33-34)*

Many people at the time of Christ wrongly assumed that the result of Christ's rise in prominence was to establish an earthly type of kingdom, one in which Christ was to sit on His throne and rule and operate the same way as earthly kingdoms do. Those closest to the king would receive their own positions of prominence and prestige. The disciples had this earthly interpretation of the Kingdom of God.

Jesus responds to the disciples in three ways:
1. In Matthew 20:23, Christ reminds the disciples that any position of authority is not His to give, but has been prepared by His Father.
2. He tells them that they are to become as humble as children. In Matthew 18:3, when Christ talks about the humility of a child, He reminds them of the fact that children have no achievements, accomplishments, personal means of support, wisdom, or ability to face the world. They have no ability to protect themselves. They are dependent, vulnerable, and weak. They bring nothing of any material value to the parent-child relationship.
3. Christ tells them that in order to become great they are to become servants (Matthew 20:26). Christ equates great-

ness in His Kingdom to serving (Mark 10:41-45; Luke 22:24-27; Philippians 2:3-11).

We won't go into detail of these three responses here, but suffice it to say that Christ is urging the disciples to pursue exactly the opposite of what the world considers great. I would encourage you to study each of these passages on your own as they are certainly worthy of further study.

Before we judge the disciples too harshly, we must remember that often we have the same heart. Many of us dream of being the best or achieving greatness in our careers. Olympic athletes train their entire lives for a chance to be recognized as the best in the world at their skill. Others pursue higher education to reach their goals. However, our desired career path or professional goals rarely go according to our plans because our plans are rarely in alignment with God's sovereignty.

Now, don't misunderstand me. I am not discounting the pursuit of excellence in everything we do and glorifying God in all we do (1 Corinthians 10:31). But, as Christ teaches above, pursuing greatness in God's eyes is different than pursuing greatness in men's eyes.

Here are some practical steps to deal with being passed up for a promotion:

1. Remember Christ's response to the disciples.

Positions of prominence and authority were not His to give, they were directed by the Father (Matthew 20:23).

2. Respectfully ask, "Why?"

Don't sit and speculate as to why you were not offered the promotion. Seek feedback. Ask the hiring manager or the HR manager specific reasons why you were not selected. Did you lack the necessary skill-set they were seeking? Did you not interview well? What areas can you work on to position yourself for the next role that opens up? If there are items within your control to change (e.g., education, training, different job skills), then consider addressing them. Depending on the specific feedback, seek wise counsel for verification.

3. Be prepared for the answer.

Be prepared to hear that the organization does not deem you to have the necessary skill-set to be promoted. From the company's perspective, perhaps you have achieved the highest you are perceived to be qualified for. This may or may not be true. However, this perspective is to be considered as you evaluate your career.

4. Do not respond sinfully to the decision.

This means not to grumble or complain about the organization's selection (Philippians 2:14). A sinful response to the organization's decision only validates their selection. I can recall many times where I have questioned the promotional decisions of my organization with a critical heart, and I didn't even apply for the role! A positive and future-focused response is God-honoring and places your trust in God's designed plan.

5. Reconsider your motives.

Perhaps they are selfishly motivated. Consider stepping back from applying for other positions for the near term. Try resting where God has you at the present time. If this creates anxiety for you, then perhaps your motivation is not God-centered.

6. Congratulate the co-worker who received the promotion.

Wish your co-worker well and give him or her your full support.

7. Reconsider your priorities.

Perhaps this is a time to reconsider your goals and priorities. Which is more important to you: career advancement, or using your current position to be a witness for Christ? God will put you in the best position to glorify Himself, to sanctify you, and to be His ambassador wherever He has placed you.

8. Be grateful for the job you have.

Express gratitude to God for the opportunity for work. Perhaps your motivation for desiring a promotion was out of discontent for the job you are in now. I'm guilty of this attitude, but God in His sovereignty did not release me from a particular position because of His sanctifying love for me. His desire was for me to submit to His will and start performing my current role to His glory, not my own. Thankfully, God loves us enough to not always give us what we want. This teaches us gratitude for what we do have.

9. Trust in God's sovereignty.

It could very well be that the promotion was gained because of unethical behavior on the behalf of the individual promoted or the hiring manager who offered the position. That has no bearing on your responsibility or reaction to trust in His ultimate will. Perhaps there are changes coming down the road that you don't know about. Maybe a different and better job is about to become available. Who knows? Only God does—and you can trust that He has your best interests at heart (Jeremiah 29:11).

10. Don't underestimate God's love for you.

Being passed up for a promotion in no way diminishes you in God's eyes. His ultimate authority and judgment is based on separate criteria and it is not measured by men (1 Samuel 16:7).

Focusing on God's priorities is not always easy, especially when our superiors express that another individual is measured above us. But that is not the spiritual reality. Focus on God's desire for your (and other's) spiritual growth and eternal salvation. That may or may not include the promotion you desire, but it does include His ultimate glory. We need to remind ourselves that we have the same temptation as the disciples: the desire to be great. Yet God, even knowing this, loves us deeply and sent His Son as an atoning sacrifice. Only when we realize the significance of this sacrifice will we have a childlike humility.

For Further Study

1. Read Matthew 20: 20-28. What about Jesus' response are we to take regarding being passed up for a promotion? What is the world's reaction to achieving a position of prominence? What is to be the believer's reaction?

2. What is the opposite of pursuing greatness that Jesus discussed in Matthew 18:1-4? What are the qualities that define this description?

3. Read 1 Samuel 16. How do men measure value? What is God's criteria? How are you determining another's value or worth?

4. In the Mark 9 passage above, why did Jesus ask the question? Why did the disciples remain silent?

Chapter 18

Feeling Unappreciated or Under-Employed

"I don't get paid enough for this."
"Nobody listens to me."
"I could run this place better than they can."
"Why did he get that promotion instead of me?"

ave you ever expressed those sentiments at work? I certainly have. It sounds prideful when you get down to it, doesn't it? Well, it is. It is a prideful expression of yourself, your abilities, and your perceived lack of status. You believe you deserve better than what you are getting at work, and that people should listen to you!

I remember a Human Resources role I had where I struggled with respecting a leader. He was belittling, ignorant of the role of Human Resources in the current business environment and treated people as tools to achieve his management goals. He was a bully. Others shared the same sentiments, and we had many gripe sessions of his poor leadership skills. I became extremely resentful of his behavior and was angry with him at every meeting I attended with him. Every word or position he took was an irritation that I couldn't resolve. How dare he treat me with disrespect! I dreaded any interaction with him and avoided him at all costs. As a result, I became embittered at him, my job, and God for keeping me in this toxic environment. It took a long time for me to realize that regarding my spiritual walk, the problem was with me and not him. It was how I was reacting to him and his style. It was not in a humble, loving, godly manner. I was focused on the wrong things.

Another challenge that you may be struggling with is a feeling of being "under-employed." You could very well be in a job that is strictly necessary for provision. You must provide for your family and have taken a position that is beneath your experience or education level. You could very well have the experience level and skill-set to do more within your organization. However, due to unforeseen circumstances (a job loss or being passed over for a promotion), your current position is one that you feel is beneath you. This is a humbling experience, and one that can also lead to a prideful reaction. We can become angry, embittered, and feel unappreciated. A wrong attitude could manifest itself in poor performance or even a lack of submission to authority.

While there are many manifestations of this attitude, they all have a common root. It comes down to seeking our identity and joy from our performance at work and the approval/recognition of men rather than receiving those things from our life in Christ. As a result, we refuse to accept our current situation as fair and while we won't admit it, we display a lack of submission to God and His sovereign authority in our lives. It's believing we are better than someone else in certain regards and deserve recognition for our perceived superior talents. It's ultimately putting our trust and hope in something other than Christ and seeking our worth outside of Him.

Throughout my career, I have seen many people who strive for excellence in their work, but for the wrong reasons. It's to increase their position or status, to get that promotion, or make more money. Sometimes it's to compensate for other, more disappointing aspects of their lives, like a divorce or difficult childhood that left them believing their worth is something that needs to be proven or gained. Or, in an effort to remove themselves from the pain of personal rejection, they "double-down" on their work efforts.

Again, let us remind ourselves of God's intention by introducing work to His creation. In introducing the concept of work, God invited us to participate in His creation by enjoying our God-given gifts to encourage and build the Body of Christ, to sanctify His people, for His glory.

Whenever we lose this focus, we will never fulfill God's desire for us to participate with Him in glorifying Him and enjoying His Kingdom. We will never get the proper perspective of work when we pursue worldly value or identity from what we do as a career (Genesis 3:17-19). Yet when we keep trying to gain this worth from our work performance or our boss's recognition, we will always be disappointed.

The world places value on worldly and temporal things. Remember, David was too young to even be presented to Samuel (1 Samuel 16:6-11). The Corinthians disregarded Paul's message because he was not as eloquent or persuasive in speech as others (1 Corinthians 2:1-5). We tend to measure our own worth by these same standards.

Staying focused on eternal things rather than temporal things that we must deal with on a daily basis is a difficult mind-set to develop. We must *intentionally* set our minds on eternal things. Colossians 3:1-4 states:

> *"If then you have been raised with Christ, seek the things that are above, where Christ is, seated at the right hand of God. Set your minds on things that are above, not on things that are on earth For you have died, and your life is hidden with Christ in God. When Christ who is your life appears, then you also will appear with him in glory."*

Verse 3 is key in this passage, "for you have died and your life is hidden with Christ in God." What does it mean that our life is hidden in Christ? William Hendrickson states it this way:

> "By means of His entire work of humiliation, including burial, Christ procured for you the work of the Holy Spirit. (John 16:7) Hence, yours is not only justification but also sanctification, gradual spiritual renewal. The Spirit has implanted in your hearts the seed of the new life. "You died, and your life is hid with Christ in God." Hence, also in this sense, you were buried with him and you were raised with him." [11]

This is the gospel! This is our identity! This is our joy—not in how we are recognized at work, but in the fact that Christ recognizes us! We are raised with Him and He is keeping us hidden in His heart until He comes again. Paul is telling us to "set our minds" on this. This is a profound passage. We can glean several key points.

---

11   Hendricksen, W. 1964. *Galatians, Ephesians, Philippians, Colossians, and Philemon.* Baker Academic, p.115.

- We have died and our life is not our own. It belongs to Christ. Christ paid the cost for our sin. He bore the judgment of God that we deserved. When we believed and accepted the gospel, we willingly gave our lives to Christ. (Romans 7:4)

- Our heart has become cleansed. Christ will not assume any sin. Our lives and hearts are cleansed by His blood in order to be "in Him." Christ's heart is our heart. Our hearts are pure as Christ holds our life in Him. (Hebrews 9:11-14)

- Christ is the caretaker and protector of our lives. There is no better protector than the Creator God Himself. No stronghold can penetrate Him to take our lives from within Him. (John 17:6-12)

- We will be revealed when Christ is revealed. Christ will reveal that He has been holding our lives within Him on the last Day, when judgment comes, and He restores His Kingdom on earth. We are children of God. We will reign with the Creator God in this Kingdom as joint heirs (Romans 8:17).

- It is finished! (John 19:30) Christ's work on the cross is finished and He holds our salvation within Himself. There is no need for us to prove our worth to anyone, or to gain it from anyone. Christ has determined our worth by sacrificing Himself on the cross for our sins. This is an eternal worth!

So, how can we practically apply these eternal truths in our workplace? Remember:

1. Any talents you have come directly from God.

They are for His glory, and He can do with them as He wishes. His priorities for us (and others) are eternal and not temporal. In His provision of gifts and talents, He is molding us into His image and not satisfying our "fleshly desires." He is furthering His Kingdom with His distribution of gifts and talents, not ours.

2. Drop the expectations of others.

Why do you expect to receive approval from men? Every person has their own set of expectations. Discontentment occurs when our expectations of others are not met. We are hindered in our ability to love others due to our expectations of them.

3. Don't forget where your hope lies.

Our hope lies in the body and blood of Jesus Christ, not on money, status, or position. As the popular saying goes, "We live in the 'already'... and the 'not yet.'" Our hope has already been accomplished on the cross and Christ is holding our eternal life in His bosom until He returns. This is our eternal hope!

4. Live your life as it is hidden in Christ.

You have been bought. You are not your own anymore. You have given your life to Christ to hold and protect as He sees fit . . . or have you really? There is a gratitude and joy that comes in knowing that our lives are securely protected within the King of Kings. Live with an eternal gratitude and joy for your salvation.

5. Develop habits that focus you on the mind of Christ.

What are your first thoughts in the morning or last thoughts at night? What are your priorities throughout the day? My wife and I enrolled in a theological training class at our church. One of the books that we studied is *The Common Rule* by Justin Whitmel Earley. This is an extremely helpful tool in determining what temporal things are distracting us from placing Christ as the priority in our lives and how to develop habits to correct this.

J.I. Packer, in his book, *Knowing God* states,

"Do I, as a Christian, understand myself? Do I know my own real identity? My own real destiny? I am a child of God. God is my Father; heaven is my home; every day is one day nearer. My Savior is my brother; every Christian is my brother too. Say it over and over to yourself first thing in the morning, last thing at night, as your wait for the bus, any time your mind is free, and ask that you may be enabled to live as one who knows it is all utterly and completely true. For this is the Christian's secret of—a happy life?—yes, certainly, but we have something both higher and profounder to say. This is the Christian's secret of a Christian life and of a God-honoring life, and these are the aspects of the situation that really matter. May this secret become fully yours, and fully mine."[12]

Our worth is not on the appreciation we get from others or having a job that we believe is worthy of our skills, abilities, or education. Our worth is in Christ, our eternal salvation. God considered us worthy to send His son to die for our sins. There is no need to seek our worth from anyone or anything else other than in the love of Jesus Christ for us. "Rejoice in the Lord always, and again I will say, rejoice!" (Philippians 4:4).

---

12   Packer, J. I. 1973. *Knowing God.* InterVarsity Press, p. 224.

For Further Study

1. Describe a work situation where you have felt unappreciated. What led to this and how did you react?
2. Read Isaiah 53:3 and Matthew 21:42. Who else was unappreciated? What did He continually focus on through this?
   What can we learn from this?
3. Read Philippians 4:4-9. What do we rejoice in? What are we
   to dwell on in our thoughts? How can we do that?
4. Read 1 Corinthians 1:18-2:16. Why is the world's wisdom
   foolishness to God? How do we obtain the mind of God?

Chapter 19

Workplace Stress

t's important to address the issue of feeling stressed in the workplace, because more of us deal with it than we care to admit. We may hesitate to discuss it with close Christian brothers and sisters because we don't want to be seen as weak-minded or of little faith. But, not confronting our stress only results in building resentment that can't help but impact our personal lives and relationships, especially our relationship with our loving God. This doesn't have to be the case if we maintain a biblical perspective.

Many things cause us to feel stressed or overwhelmed with our work and they vary by situation and individual. It could be the volume of work, a lack of resources, or perhaps a fear of losing employment. Maybe you're a people pleaser. You want to do a good job so others will think well of you, but there may be times where you let others down. Maybe you have an unreasonable boss, and you have difficulty meeting his or her expectations.

A feeling of inadequacy happens when we are dealing with limited knowledge or skills to accomplish a task. Rather than address these gaps directly and take steps to correct them, we can become angry, dejected, or even despondent, falling into sin. I personally tend to be a perfectionist and want every "i" dotted, every "t" crossed, and every base covered. (That's a pride and control issue, by the way.)

In Philippians 4, Scripture commands us to not be anxious, and to present our requests to God with a grateful heart, assuring us that, through Christ, He will provide the peace that only He can give.

> *"Do not be anxious about anything, but in everything by prayer and supplication with thanksgiving let your requests be made known to God. And the peace of God, which surpasses all understanding, will guard your hearts and your minds in Christ Jesus." (Philippians 4:6-7)*

This same passage goes on to tell us to focus our very thoughts on eternal and godly things:

> *"Finally, brothers, whatever is true, whatever is honorable, whatever is just, whatever is pure, whatever is lovely, whatever is commendable, if there is any excellence, if there is anything worthy of praise, think about these things. What you have learned and received and heard and seen in me—practice these things, and the God of peace will be with you." (Philippians 4:8-9)*

This passage has guided me through some stressful situations by encouraging me to think eternally and not allow my emotions to control my actions. Right thinking leads to right actions.

So, what are some actions we can take when we are experiencing an overwhelming and stressful work situation?

1. Share your struggles with others.

Confessing sin to fellow believers reminds us of how far from perfect we all are. You will be surprised at how similar our spiritual battles are when real fellowship occurs. Encouragement will follow.

2. Focus on what really matters.

Preach the gospel to yourself every morning. Study the Word daily, read devotions throughout the day, and pray without ceasing. Listen to worship music. Post Scripture verses and encouraging/inspiring quotes where you can see them. Listen to sermons or biblical podcasts on your commute or while you are going about your mundane daily tasks. These simple steps help refocus our minds on Christ.

3. Praise and worship God for who He is.

Read a Psalm to remind yourself of the mighty power of a holy God, the creator and savior of all eternity. Only through this can we truly be grateful for the grace, mercy and love He extends to us, even amid workplace trials. (Psalm 118)

4. Remember to work diligently for God's approval and not man's.

You will never receive man's unconditional approval, so stop trying. A desire to please people is a fear of man. This is a snare because we can never please men enough and hence we will always be anxious about what our boss thinks of us or of losing our job. We are to do excellent work and exceed our boss's expectations, not for their approval but to honor God. (Proverbs 29:25; Ephesians 6:5-8; Colossians 3:23-24)

5. Use the resources that are available.

If you are feeling inadequate or overwhelmed because of a lack of knowledge in a particular area, use your resources, such as subject matter experts. If you don't have any resources, find some! Take classes or go back to school. Be diligent and persistent and slowly you will master the task and become a subject matter expert yourself.

6. Recognize your stress threshold.

This is something critical that I had to learn. When you get to the point where you become anxious or stressed about your work or a work situation, recognize that point immediately. Don't fall into the trap of working harder to decrease the anxiety because it never works. Stop, step back, and pray. Pray fervently, seek God in His Word, and counsel with others. Confess, repent, and truly present your cares to Christ.

7. Make a daily list of items that need to be accomplished.

Accomplish what you can within the time frame you have without falling into the sin of anxiety, and then give the rest to God. This is not a license to procrastinate or be lazy. (Proverbs 26:12-16; 2 Thessalonians 3:6-10; 1 Timothy 5:8) Things that you are not able to accomplish today, carry over to tomorrow's list.

8. Prioritize the list.

Work on the things that demand a sense of importance or urgency. Your superiors may direct these, or you may be empowered to evaluate the levels of importance on your own. If so, determine what items have the most impact. One of my favorite sayings is, "A high level of activity doesn't necessarily mean forward progress." Develop long-term goals and prioritize your list accordingly.

9. Focus on one thing at a time.

In this age of constant and immediate communication and expectations, it is easy to be distracted and not completely focus on doing excellent work on the task at hand. You must be more disciplined in taking ownership of your mind and your time. It's easy to be tempted by outside distractions while you work. For example, if you are stocking shelves in a store, it's tempting to be on your phone or checking text messages to pass the time. Honor God by honoring your employer. Resist the urge to check email and voice mail every time you hear the alert (especially if you are on a date with your wife—trust me on this one!). There is nothing wrong with putting your phone on "Do Not Disturb" and checking messages at a more appropriate time.

10. Expect changes, obstacles, roadblocks, and interruptions.

Some distractions are legitimate work situations that require urgent attention while others are of a more personal nature. God in His sovereignty brings many different circumstances in our lives at unexpected times. Expect them and this decreases the temptation to become angry and frustrated when they occur. These are sanctifying opportunities and perhaps even gospel opportunities.

11. Pace yourself.

Don't try to solve world hunger and attempt to fix everything at the same time. That's impossible. Make one decision at a time and you will make the appropriate progress.

12. Thank God.

Step back and express sincere gratitude to God for the employment He has provided you. We are naturally discontent with our

circumstances. Speaking from first-hand experience, being unem-
ployed is much more stressful than any workplace issue that I had
to deal with on a daily basis.

13. Remember your identity is in Christ and not in the work you do.
(2 Corinthians 5:17; Ephesians1:11-14; Colossians 3:1-4)

These are just a few ideas to address the specific issues that we
may find overwhelming or stressful in our workplace. If we do not
recognize and deal with these issues, we will eventually become
angry and bitter toward our work, our boss, and our employer.
This bitterness eventually rolls over into our personal lives, and we
may find ourselves ultimately shaking our fist at the circumstances
that God has providentially ordained. This is a dangerous place for
us spiritually because it is rebellion against God Himself. Wherever we want to lay the blame of workplace stress and anxiety, it
comes down to one single thing: our own sinful nature.

Jesus Christ offers to remove the overwhelming stress of our
lives by taking it upon Himself. There is peaceful rest in giving our
entire lives, including our work, over to Him.

> *"Come to me, all who labor and are heavy laden, and I will give
> you rest. Take my yoke upon you, and learn from me, for I am
> gentle and lowly in heart, and you will find rest for your souls. For
> my yoke is easy, and my burden is light." (Matthew 11: 28-30)*

These words of our Lord remind us that He came to free us
from the labor and burden of the ceremonial law, the law that we
can never work hard enough to fulfill. But in our attempts, we
will not recognize the depth and burden of our sin that manifests

itself in continued anxiety, stress, and weariness in our lives, and we will continue to labor against it, harder and harder every day. Christ lovingly urges us to come to Him and willingly submit to his Lordship. If we do, He promises that His burdens are easy and light. Recognize that the struggles you experience at work are because of not trusting and submitting to Christ. Go to His open arms, even run to Him. Allow Him to remove this burden from you and enjoy the peace that only He can give.

For Further Study

1. Read Matthew 6:25-34. What does God know about our needs and how does He know them? Why do we become anxious about these needs and what does our anxiety really display? Distinguish between needs and wants.

2. Read Ephesians 6: 12-20. Is our battle truly against our workplace? What tools does Christ give us to engage in spiritual battle?

3. Read Philippians 4:8-9 and 1 Peter 1:13. What happens if we allow our emotions to rule our minds? What are we to focus our minds on and put our hope in?

4. How does anxiety and stress relate to our spiritual sanctification? (See Romans 5:1-5 and James 1:2-4.)

5. Read Psalm 142, written by David. David spent many stressful days and nights fleeing for his life from King Saul. What can we learn from this psalm?

6. When we question or complain about our stressful circumstances, it would be helpful to remind ourselves of who God is and who we are. Read chapters 38-41 from the Book of Job. Do we have a right to question any of God's sovereignty in our lives?

Chapter 20

Work / Life Balance

n today's hectic work environment, it's popular to encourage a
certain separation of work and life that will supposedly allow
individuals to have the best of both worlds without one negatively impacting the other. This is the myth of work/life balance.
It presumes that our work lives and personal lives are mutually
exclusive. It operates under the false assumption that we can leave
the worries of our personal life at home and the stress and anxiety of our daily work diminishes when we clock out for the day.
I believe that is a difficult, if not impossible, goal—a goal that I
believe tends to increase one's anxiety level rather than alleviate it.

Let me illustrate this with a personal example. When my father
passed away, it was very sudden, and our family was not prepared
emotionally or practically to deal with an unexpected death. I
was out of town on a business trip and dropped everything to be
with my mother and siblings. The concept of work/life balance
suddenly falls apart in this type of circumstance. If I subscribed
to a work/life balance lifestyle, then it stands to reason that after
the funeral, I should be able to separate the circumstances of my

father's death from my work duties and focus intently on being productive. That's impractical. It was impossible for me to separate my work from my personal life during the grieving process and go back to the life I'd had just a few short days prior. I needed to adjust my priorities.

A work/life balance coach may grant an exception in these types of life-altering situations. But there are many difficult life situations that can affect us deeply and have long-term impact. What about those with a difficult marriage or who are going through a divorce? What about parents who are struggling with a rebellious child? Or perhaps the loss of a child? What about a serious medical or health issue with yourself or a loved one? What about those struggling financially and worrying about paying the rent?

We cannot separate our personal lives and our work lives. They are intrinsically linked. We think about work things at home and personal things at work. We live one life, not two (or even more) mutually exclusive lives.

Christ addresses a double-minded lifestyle in the book of Matthew:

"No one can serve two masters, for either he will hate the one and love the other, or he will be devoted to the one and despise the other. You cannot serve God and money." (Matthew 6:24)

We are called to live a life wholly devoted to God, with an unwavering focus on honoring our Lord and Savior with every decision we are faced with, regardless of the situation or circumstance. We cannot live separate lives that sway with the circumstances.

However, the ability or inability to manage our work/life balance is not the primary issue. Even if we occasionally have some degree of success, we will never be able to separate our personal and work lives completely, nor should we. Scripture never commands us to live separate, worldly lives. Rather, Christ commands us to live our lives separately from the world. We need to cease striving to separate our daily lives into compartments and attempting to balance two things that will never be in balance anyway. Instead, we should seek to bring a singular, focused effort to all that we do—a singular focus on Christ. Paul states this very clearly in Colossians 3:1-4:

"If then you have been raised with Christ, seek the things that are above, where Christ is, seated at the right hand of God. Set your minds on things that are above, not on things that are on earth. For you have died, and your life is hidden with Christ in God. When Christ who is your life appears, then you also will appear with him in glory."

Paul is commanding us to "set our hearts and minds" on things above, not on things of this world. The word "set" here is "to be intent on." This is a single focus, nothing separate here. This completely eliminates the need for any "work/life balance." We are to focus on Christ at every moment, no matter where we are or what we are doing. We are to focus on His redemptive work in our personal lives and in our professional lives.

Jesus did not live a life of seeking work/life balance. His redemptive work and His continuing, sanctifying work to redeem us and mold us into His image is His singular focus. His sovereign work in our lives is to that end alone. We must keep this one thing in the forefront of our minds in every situation He brings to our work or personal lives.

However, having a life that focuses on Christ may manifest itself in some surprising ways in the workplace. Here's another personal example. For several weeks, I was really looking forward to a men's conference at our church. But, some last-minute work obligations came up that were in conflict with the conference. I was extremely disappointed. I spent almost an hour looking for ways to accomplish my work obligations and allow me to attend the conference. I considered same-day airline flights and driving four hours after the conference ended at 10 p.m. for an 8 a.m. meeting the next day and other options. I finally realized that even though attending the conference was going to be a time of great fellowship and a wonderful opportunity to learn how to study God's Word, I could not do both. I decided to listen to the conference later online and fulfill my work obligations.

Initially, I caught myself being upset that God did not work it out to allow me to attend this conference. Surely He would rather me attend this conference than go to work! Now I realize that even though attending the conference was supposedly the "noble" and "God-honoring" decision, it was actually more selfish on my part. Being obedient to God was more important.

This may seem counter-intuitive on the surface, but God has called me to be His witness in my personal and professional life. That is to be my priority regardless of what I would prefer to do, even attend a Christian conference. I realized I needed to refocus my thoughts on honoring Christ with my life and work and not seek to satisfy my personal wants and desires.

So, how can we deal with work-life balance from a biblical perspective?

1. **Recognize that we cannot separate our work and personal lives.**
Stop trying to do so. You will only frustrate yourself in the attempt. We are not designed to shut down thoughts and emotions at will at any given moment.

2. **The effort to separate a personal and professional life creates a tremendous amount of stress.**
Recognize when you are starting to feel the pressure. It's vitally important at this point that you reorient yourself to God's sovereignty. If you are starting to operate from a position of stress, then you are attempting to outpace God and frantically focusing on completing the task at hand rather than honoring God with a peaceful heart. (Philippians 4:6-7)

3. **As a believer, we have one life.**
This is a life that focuses on Christ, on who He is and what He has done, and applying this to our lives every day. (Colossians 3:1-4; Hebrews 12:2)

4. **Learn to prioritize from God's point of view.**
Many times, God is teaching us to prioritize our time rather than attempting to accomplish everything. Make a single list of professional and personal things that need to be done. Honor your employer and don't use work time to accomplish personal tasks unless absolutely necessary. There will still be periods when you will need to spend an inordinate amount of time on professional or personal tasks, but that is still prioritizing your life based on Christ's objectives and not your own. Any time you fail to prioritize your whole life with a singular focus on Christ results in

failing to honor His sovereign, redemptive work. This becomes a self-discipline issue, not a work/life balance issue.

5. Don't swing to extremes.

Our tendency is to swing from one extreme to the other, which is still an attempt at work /life balance. We may use the call to "work unto the Lord" as an excuse to overwork or we may use our "God-given family responsibilities" to excuse us from doing the work that we truly should be doing. Many times, we prioritize our work over the most important people in our lives and many other times we have neglect our work and use our family as an excuse. That alone proves that it is impossible to separate life and work.

6. Practice self-discipline.

We fall into sinful habits when we fail to lead a singular, Christ-centered life. We are too afraid of missing something at work, so we are constantly checking emails and even responding to them outside of work hours or on vacation. Sometimes we allow personal, family drama to consume our workday. Having a life focused on Christ and seeking His glory is the solution to this as we seek to do all things to the glory of God. We should practice self-discipline in these areas and address situations at the appropriate times.

One thing that personal trials have been teaching me at this point in my life (including the passing of my father) is that I cannot live my life separate from Christ. I need to focus on Him daily or even more, moment by moment, just to remind myself that Christ is the first and *only* thing.

We are created to live one life, not two—one singular spiritual life. It is impossible for us to operate in two separate worlds, with two separate mindsets, with two separate life goals. We were never intended to live our lives outside of the giver of life itself. Jesus Christ is the source of eternal life; where else can we go?

For Further Study

1. Read Philippians 4. Detail the characteristics of a heavenly mindset.

2. Read Colossians 3:1-17. What are we to put off and what are we to put on? Why and how are we to do that? How does this create a single-focused mindset?

3. Read 1 Thessalonians 5:16-18. How does this relate to living a life focused on Christ?

Chapter 21

Lack of Motivation

I must confess: There have been many times throughout my life and career that I have lacked motivation to work for my employer as diligently as I am called to do. I use a variety of reasons to justify this sinful attitude: My boss is not respectable or supportive, I feel undervalued, the work is boring or has no purpose, they only focus on the "bottom line," I'm not progressing in my career, or this is not what I wanted to do with my life. I'm sure that you have some of your own that you have expressed to co-workers, friends, and relatives to justify your lack of motivation. However, no excuse that we can rationalize provides a way out of our responsibility to God in our workplace. A lack of motivation reveals that our motivation is severely misplaced. Paul writes:

> "Bondservants, obey in everything those who are your earthly masters, not by way of eye-service, as people-pleasers, but with sincerity of heart, fearing the Lord. Whatever you do, work heartily, as for the Lord and not for men, knowing that from the Lord you will receive the inheritance as your reward. You are serving

the Lord Christ. For the wrongdoer will be paid back for the wrong
he has done, and there is no partiality." (Colossians 3:22-25)

I love Paul's continual focus on Christ, on who He is and what
He's done. In this section of Colossians, Paul confronts us in a
variety of earthly roles, both within the home (as husbands, wives,
parents, and as children) and outside the home (as bondservants
and masters). Paul uses the term "bondservant" here (some trans-
lations use "slave") not to condone any type of forced or even
voluntary servitude that was prevalent during that time, but to
address the matter of godly integrity and a heart of humble submission to authority (1 Peter 2:18-21).

We are to live and act in stark contrast to the world, to point
to Christ's example of humble submission to the Father in all circumstances because, our sinful flesh resists and fights against all
authority in our lives. As employees, we are bound to our employers in much the same way. To maintain our livelihood and provide
for our families, we must obey the expectations of our employer.
Hence, we are in essence willing "bondservants" to the person and
company we choose to work for.

Paul is challenging us to pursue excellence in our work, not
perform the work with a "check- the-box" type of mentality, or
merely go through the motions. He exhorts us to have a true heart
motivation, literally "from the soul," to perform our work as if the
Lord is our employer. Dr. David Jeremiah comments on this:

> "Against the backdrop of people who avoid work, cut corners,
> and do half-hearted jobs, a diligent man stands out. Practicing
> diligence is an excellent way to stand out for Christ at home, in
> the workplace, and even at church. Today, complete each one of
> your tasks, however big or small, with diligence."

A worldly attitude toward work could manifest itself in either seeking to serve our own best interests or ways to avoid it altogether. You may have a legitimate reason and motivation to work hard, such as providing for your family's future, and that's a good reason. However, a godly attitude towards work takes that energy and focuses it on pleasing God. We are to honor Christ, not people in our work ethic. That is a higher standard than merely meeting your employer's, or anyone else's, expectations. We are called to perform our work out of a sincere heart and love for Christ because, in His sovereignty, He has determined what work you are to do for Him, what lives you are to touch for His glory, and what circumstances best shape you into Christlikeness. God ordains where and for whom you are to work because He loves you and those you work with. Seeking to run from these circumstances only displays a lack of trust in His providential hand of sovereignty.

There is nothing wrong in seeking to better ourselves and our situation. That is important in our growth (both personally and professionally) and moving ourselves forward, but we need to be careful not to run from what we believe are poor circumstances, and into anything else other than the arms of our loving Savior. I can personally attest to this as I have tried many times to change my circumstances to no avail. Other times, God has intervened and has ordained to change them in the timing He determines is best, and by which He alone receives the glory.

The Lord clearly sees our heart motivation as we work for Him and will eternally reward or allow earthly consequences because of our obedience or disobedience. His eternal rewards have significantly more value than any earthly raise or promotion (Matthew 23:25-28).

So, how do we realign our motivation to work? Here are some ways:

1. Give up your pride.

Recognize that our lack of motivation stems from a prideful attitude of what we think we deserve from a worldly standpoint. In relation to God, we don't even deserve the privilege of employment, much less the position, value, and pay we think we deserve. Confess and repent of this prideful attitude. (1 John 2:16)

2. Focus on sanctification.

Focus on the God's ultimate goal: your Christlikeness, not worldly success. In the midst of a difficult situation, it's easy to forget that God has a purpose that is beyond our temporal pain and understanding (Romans 8:28-29).

3. Pray for your lost co-workers, and for opportunities to point them to Christ.

This will remind you of the eternal perspective of every aspect of our lives, even our workplace. In the secular workplace, most of your co-workers are unbelievers. We must maintain that perspective in our relationships and interaction with them.

4. Take action.

Even though you may feel unmotivated or even fearful, displaying a lack of motivation and laziness destroys our Christian witness. We are acting like unbelievers when we do this. Action feeds motivation, not the other way around. (Matthew 25:14-29)

5. Refrain from constantly voicing your displeasure.

There are times to legitimately express valid concerns regarding the workplace, but constant complaining only places the focus on you and what you want. It reveals your true heart. (Philippians 2:14-16)

6. Drop the expectations.

Remember that we live in a sinful world. Even the best bosses and employers are going to fall short of the expectations or desires we place on them. Further recognize that personal expectations and desires are sinful in and of themselves. (Romans 3:23)

7. Take joy in pleasing God in your work.

God is pleased as you take action to honor who He is. As you are obedient to Him, you are further motivated to please Him. (Hebrews 13:16)

8. Be a godly example.

Remember that God is sovereign over all creation, and He has determined who has earthly authority over you. Honor the authority that Christ has placed over you and seek to perform excellent work that pleases God. (Hebrews 13:17)

A Christ-like motivation does not come from what we think we deserve, that is our pride and flesh, but rather from Christ's love for us and our love for Him. This reveals our submission to God and trust in where He has determined to place us. I like how Charles Spurgeon put it when he said,

> "Had any other condition been better for you than the one you are in, Divine Love would have put you there."

Divine love is the key to understanding that, in His sovereignty, God has determined the circumstances of our employment, to work for His glory and our sanctification.

For Further Study

1. Read John 17. Who owns you and why?
2. If Christ were to conduct your annual performance review, what would He tell you?
3. Can you think of any ways have you dishonored God in where and for whom you worked?
4. Why do we believe we deserve the same or more than anyone else? Is life fair?
5. Read John 3:16-18. What was God's motivation? How should this change our perspective of work?

Chapter 22

Workplace Weariness

When I began digging deeper into this issue of weariness in the workplace, I underestimated the ultimate path it would take. There are multiple definitions and levels of weariness. There is physical, mental, and spiritual weariness. There is weariness that can be classified as being tired after a long day at work. Weariness can be a level of spiritual depression. There is also a weariness that comes from long-term workplace stress. (There are similarities between the two but enough of a difference to warrant another post; see also Chapter 19: Workplace Stress.)

Physical weariness due to strenuous activity is arguably the easiest to remedy, provided the time is given to recover. Scripture is clear in pointing out that physical rest is important. The primary example of this is that God rested on the seventh day and instituted a day of rest for us. (Genesis 2:1-3). In 1 Kings, Elijah fled for his life from Jezebel and God tended to him for 40 days and 40 nights to provide rest for him (1 Kings 19:1-8). Also, during this time, an angel of the Lord made an interesting statement, recorded in verse 7, "Arise, eat, because the journey is too great for you." What a great reminder that we cannot rely on our own strength! God cares for us and provides us with the physical and spiritual sustenance to persevere in times of trials. In His earthly body, even Jesus needed physical rest and sustenance (Mark 4:35-41; Luke 8:22-25).

However, physical weariness beyond our control, perhaps due to a long-term physical ailment or the daily demands of a physical job, are more difficult to address, as are the mental, emotional, and spiritual toll that trials and situations can take on a believer.

Workplace weariness can find its root in a variety of issues: a desire to control circumstances or people, a hope for a positive project outcome, a fear or anxiety of an upcoming event, juggling multiple urgent priorities, dealing with difficult co-workers or situations, constantly meeting tight deadlines, and many others. However, workplace weariness it is not primarily due to our workplace circumstances. We become weary when we focus on what we want/desire and our failure to achieve these things. Or, we focus on the things we would rather "not do." It all comes down to a focus on ourselves.

I must confess, I sometimes struggle with becoming anxious and weary about work situations. In my selfish pride, I have made an idol of seeking a quiet and peaceful life, one that will never be achieved this side of heaven. A quiet and peaceful life does not hinge on controlling our situations, circumstances, or co-workers, but resting completely in the One who does (James 1:2-4; 1 Peter 1:6-9).

The primary focus during these levels and periods of weariness can be found in the words of Christ himself:

"Come to me, all who labor and are heavy laden, and I will give you rest. Take my yoke upon you, and learn from me, for I am gentle

and lowly in heart, and you will find rest for your souls. For my yoke is easy, and my burden is light." (Matthew 11:28-30)

Growing heavy laden in labor is the Greek word *egkakeo*—"to lose heart or become discouraged." In this passage, Christ is speaking to the Jews regarding the improper application of the Law that the Pharisees have undertaken to remain in a position of power over the people. The Pharisees used the Law to burden the Jewish people, and to appease God by their adherence to the Mosaic Law. In Christ, the Law is fulfilled, and God is appeased through Christ's work of salvation on the cross, not our own efforts. Christ offers us the gift of His work to appease God for our sin ("atonement") and provide reconciliation to God and eternal life with Him for those that accept it.

In Christ's illustration above, we are the oxen, but Christ guides us and eases the burden of the yolk. He is the one that carries the load for us. Christ is urging, even pleading with us, to trust in Him and His work, not rely on ourselves or our "works-based" efforts. These are the very things that cause spiritual weariness.

Frankly, it comes down to the correct theology of God, by remembering God's purpose for our work. Honestly, I would argue that workplace weariness is more of a choice than we realize and thus is more of a spiritual condition than a physical one. There is one key difference between working hard and working to the point of exhaustion and weariness: that is remembering, focusing on, and resting in the work of Christ.

In his excellent book, *Spiritual Depression*, Dr. Martin Lloyd Jones encourages, even admonishes us, to focus more on Christ than ourselves. He rightly states that what causes weariness is a loss of focus and a lack of controlling our thoughts. He states,

"I say that we must talk to ourselves instead of allowing 'ourselves' to talk to us . . . Have you realized that most of your unhappiness in life is due to the fact that you are listening to yourself instead of talking to yourself? The main art in the matter of spiritual living is to know how to handle yourself. You have to take yourself in hand, you have to address yourself, preach to yourself, question yourself (see Matthew 22:37; Romans 8:5-7, 12:2; Colossians 3:1-4)." [13]

Lloyd-Jones continues to explain that the Great Deceiver is quick to speak lies to us and we must not listen to him, we must battle his lies with the truth. This truth is the gospel of Christ. Jesus Christ paid the price to redeem us from our sinful selves to an eternal life with Him. As a former pastor of mine used to say, "We must preach the gospel to ourselves daily." We are to live this truth every moment of every day and we must trust God that He will achieve His work (Philippians 1:6). His work is our sanctification and His glory (1 Thessalonians 4:3). Our job is to be faithful, obedient, and humble despite our circumstances (Philippians 2:12-13).

It is vitally important that we maintain this perspective in our daily work, for we never know the impact we are having on God's Kingdom and on people's lives, in spite of the difficult work situations we are experiencing.

This reminds me of the story of a medical missionary, Dr. William Leslie. In 1912, Dr. Leslie went to live and minister to a remote tribal people of the Democratic Republic of Congo. He ministered to them for 17 years. However, after a falling out

---

13   Jones, M. Lloyd. 1965. *Spiritual Depression*. William B. Erdmans Publishing, p. 20-21.

with tribal leadership, he was asked to leave and never come back. Although they eventually reconciled, Dr. Leslie returned to the U.S. a disheartened and discouraged man. He died nine years later, always believing he failed to make an impact for Christ to this remote tribe.

However, in 2010, another missionary team made a shocking and sensational discovery. They found a surprising network of churches scattered throughout the dense jungle across the Kwilu River from Vanga, where Dr. Leslie was stationed and lived. This missionary team reported that each church had its own gospel choir that wrote their own songs and would have sing-offs from village to village. This team also found a 1000-seat stone "amphitheater" in one of the villages and learned that the church got so crowded in the 1980s that a church planting movement began to the surrounding areas. Even though Dr. Leslie did not live to see it, God used the efforts of a discouraged, disheartened, weary man to bring the eternal truth of the gospel to thousands of His people in the Congo who initially rejected it.

How do we do that, especially in a workplace where there are people who either disregard or even reject any biblical or Christian teaching? Here are a few things to remember:

1. Work hard, but remember that God controls the results.

We are called to work hard and do it with excellence, but God is sovereign over the outcome. Even though we may become discouraged, weary, and disheartened, God's perspective is always good. (John 16:33; Colossians 3:23)

2. We are not in control of other's behaviors.

We can anticipate and prepare for them the best we can, but no one is within our control. I still have a tendency to react negatively to frivolous lawsuits brought to the organization, but I need to remember that I cannot control when people want to sue the organization in an attempt to get a windfall of money. We live in a fallen world and "sinners will be sinners." Even as believers, we are still sinners, and unbelievers have no capacity or motivation to act any other way. We cannot expect anything different. As a former Bible teacher of my wife's used to say, "They (unbelievers) are only doing what they are supposed to be doing." (Romans 14:1-23, 16: 17-18; 2 Timothy 3:1-5)

3. Things will never be perfect.

Try as I might to manipulate my circumstances to be perfect and comfortable, they never will be. There will always be something else or someone else who (in my opinion) needs "fixing." Who am I to say that my opinion of circumstances is the right one, anyway? Doesn't God know what circumstances are best? My attempts to manipulate my world and the people in it are prideful and futile at best. (Romans 14:1-23)

4. You cannot meet everyone's expectations.

That alone will drive you to weariness. I am not perfect. I tend to try and meet everyone's expectations from the Board of Directors on down and am concerned about letting others down and having someone in authority being upset with me. That is simply a fear of man. (Proverbs 29:25)

5. We are not in control of our circumstances.

We cannot control outcomes of situations. Even if things go according to our plan, the outcome is God's alone. He has already chosen what outcome He desires, and we are feeble in our attempts to change it.

6. We must not be afraid to confront sinful behavior.

Avoidance is surprisingly emotionally and spiritually draining. This causes weariness. Christ gives us a pattern of confronting sin in Matthew 18:15-20. In 2 Thessalonians 3:10-15, Paul gives us a command to confront undisciplined individuals by not giving in to their associations and admonishing them as brothers and sisters in Christ. (See Chapter 9: "Managing Poor Performance.")

7. Take a step back.

The world will not fall apart if you back off from trying to be and do everything. I hate to be the bearer of bad news, but you are not the glue that holds the world together! (Colossians 1:15-17).

8. Focus on the big, impactful things.

Prioritize the most important or urgent things. It's easy to become distracted in the cares of this world. (Matthew 13:22).

9. Don't focus on your own discouragement; focus on God's objectives.

Remember that it is not about us; it is about God's sanctifying work in our lives. His desire is to conform us more to the image of Christ. (Romans 8:28-29).

10. Focus on and rest in Christ and persevere in His love for you.

Remind yourself daily of God's sovereignty and His love for you through all circumstances. (James 1:12; 2 Peter 1:6-9)

We are called to not grow weary of doing good work and honoring God in our efforts. God will reward our faithful efforts of obedience to Him. We are to remember our purpose with perseverance and trust in the power of God. Primarily, honoring, and obeying God, and following Him in His steps in everything we do is the key to not growing weary. This is part of how we "work out" our salvation and live out the good news of the gospel before those who are lost. (Philippians 3:14)

For Further Study

1. Read Philippians 4:5-6. Where is God in your situation? What are the implications of this and how does this impact your reaction?

2. Read Hebrews 12:3-17. Compare your current weariness to the suffering described in this passage.

3. Read 2 Thessalonians 3:10-15. Paul commands the Thessalonians to not grow weary of doing good. What is happening and what is the good that is occurring in this passage? How can the Thessalonians not grow weary? Note how not growing weary is a command. Does that mean it is within our control?

4. Read Galatians 6:6-10. Should we be working for ourselves or for the glory of Christ? What might this look like in your own circumstances?

5. Read Psalm 131. What should we *not* focus on, and where instead is our rest and peace?

Chapter 23

Escaping from Work

certainly realize that escapism is more of a topic than a specific workplace issue, but after reflecting on this in my own life, I realized that it has implications that manifest itself in specific ways regarding the workplace. It has for me.

Now, there is a difference between taking a break and escaping or avoiding. We all work hard at our jobs, and it is totally appropriate to take a break from the hard work every now and then. We are still commanded to rest. This is not what I am referring to. I am referring to the deliberate avoidance of dealing with workplace obligations or circumstances.

As a result of our original sin, we were cursed with the fact that work, in general, will be difficult (Genesis 3:17-19). Dealing with our own sin or the sins of others is mentally, emotionally. and physically exhausting.

I realize that I have spent an inordinate amount of my time trying to escape the "thorns and thistles," or consequences, of this curse in my own work life. Some of the things that I have sought escape from are: the bullying management style of a boss, frustration of workplace politics, anger at employees who try and manipulate the system for their own gain, weariness of the work pace, or jealously comparing my cultural lifestyle to others who are "further along" than I am.

Some ways that I have attempted to escape this curse is by entertainment or isolation. I have watched so many television series or movies that my wife often asks, "When did you watch *that*?" I would isolate myself during lunch times or catch a few minutes at slower times during the day as a break. When waking up in the middle of the night I would watch a show or two before falling back to sleep to relieve the flood of anxious thoughts of work that keep me awake. There is nothing wrong with taking some time for play or spending alone time, but when it becomes a too-often attempt to escape difficult or challenging situations, then it is destructive to our spiritual condition.

Another escape is to dream of financial independence. I confess to have played the lottery on occasion and rested in the hope of all the numbers hitting. What peace that would bring! I have used that dream money to buy all the comfort and security that the world has to offer and escape the difficulty of work. That would certainly eliminate any more "bad bosses" or difficult workplace issues! But the numbers have never hit and then, of course, reality overcomes false hope. I also thought I would start personally investing in the stock market in hopes of buying low into the next Bitcoin or Amazon. But those numbers never hit either.

I was doing great work from a worldly standpoint, but I was seeking my identity in my work relationships rather than my identity in Christ. When my work relationships were not collaborative relationships that fit my own style, I became embittered. It wasn't meeting my own prideful expectations. My spiritual attitude toward work changed and therefore I was not doing excellent work for the glory of God.

Other worldly attempts that many people (including professing believers) use to escape may include alcohol, sports, drugs, sex or pornography, social media, video games, shopping, hobbies, and countless other distractions. Some attempts to escape may have well-meaning goals and intentions and are not necessarily "bad" activities in and of themselves. Nonetheless, when used in this way, they can be destructive to our spiritual lives.

It's easy to become discouraged at the amount of "thorns and thistles" that we have to deal with on a day-to-day basis in our workplace, but escaping from them is never in God's plan.

Our first reaction to difficult circumstances reveals much about our spiritual condition and where our hope lies. For most of us, it is a desire to remove ourselves from the situation, to make it go away. We avoid conflict. We procrastinate and deflect. When escape or avoidance is the first place we run to instead of into the arms of our loving God and protector, then we never really escape. We just start a never-ending cycle of self-perpetuating suffering.

The attitude that is at the root of escaping, delaying, or avoiding difficult work situations is the seeking of pleasure and temporarily avoiding the painful reality of these difficult situations. In actuality, we are avoiding God's sovereign purposes in our lives. This is simply an act of rebellion against the sovereignty of God and a lack of trust in His desire for us. We have made an idol of worldly ease and comfort rather than seeking spiritual growth.

The Bible warns us about this very attitude:

"But understand this, that in the last days there will come times of difficulty. For people will be lovers of self, lovers of money, proud, arrogant, abusive, disobedient to their parents, ungrateful, unholy,

heartless, unappeasable, slanderous, without self-control, brutal, not loving good, treacherous, reckless, swollen with conceit, lovers of pleasure rather than lovers of God, having the appearance of godliness, but denying its power. Avoid such people." (2 Timothy 3:1-5)

We can certainly discuss this list in detail, but, granted, it is not an all-inclusive list. An abundance of drugs and the availability of social media were certainly not escape options in Paul's time. There are many ungodly pursuits and distractions that are not listed here. An all-inclusive list is not Paul's point. Our desire to seek comfort in something other than God is what he is getting at.

The phrases that impacted me the most in this passage are warning us about being lovers of pleasure rather than lovers of God, and indicating that we may appear godly but in reality deny His power. Seekers of pleasure make a "show" of religion and assume a form of godliness to take away any worldly reproach, but they will not submit to the power of the gospel to take away their sin and provide the comfort that they desperately seek. One commentator states: "A form of godliness is a very different thing than the power of it; men may have the one and be wholly destitute of the other."[14]

Running to various escapes is only a temporary bandage to our larger problem. Much like using alcohol to numb your pain or playing the lottery and dreaming of a more comfortable life, these are only temporary distractions and, when our dreams are denied, we must once again face reality. It drives us into an even deeper resentment. If we are using anything other than God's comfort to avoid the difficulties of our work lives, then we are attempting to escape the sovereignty of God. We have become

---

14   *Matthew Henry's Commentary.* Peabody, MA: Hendrickson Publishers, pg. 680.

lovers of self and have forgotten our first love (Revelation 2:4). As Eugene Peterson writes:

> "Without worship we live manipulated and manipulating lives. We move in either frightened panic or deluded lethargy as we are, in turn, alarmed by specters and soothed by placebos." [15]

"Escapism" is what we call being overwhelmed by worldly issues and pursuing rest in worldly distractions other than the giver of rest. God, in His infinite love, knows that we need rest. He gives us good things for our rest. But even pursuing God's provisions of rest outside of Him, or at the wrong time or in the wrong quantity, only leads to worshiping the provision rather than the provider. We then blame God for not providing the rest as we define it. We seek rest in the pursuit of comfort or control rather than resting in God's loving comfort and sovereignty. This misguided pursuit becomes an idol of our heart and leads to the same disappointing outcome.

With all that in mind, what are some ways to address escapism? Here are some suggestions:

1. Ask yourself some probing questions.

What am I trying to accomplish when I pursue _____? What do I hope to gain? Is it relief? Comfort? Independence? This will help you identify the idol(s) in your heart that needs to be addressed.

---

15 Peterson, E. 1988. *Reversed Thunder*. San Francisco, CA: Harper & Row, pg. 60.

2. Examine what triggers the desire to escape.

Keep a log of the times that you just want to remove yourself from your current circumstances. Is there a pattern? Keeping a journal of the times where you feel the urge to escape can be helpful if you have trouble identifying the specific things that trigger this desire. You can then determine the necessary spiritual steps to take.

3. Recognize how far away from God your road to escape has taken you.

As you become aware of the triggers that increase your desire to escape, you will realize that escaping will not take you one step closer to aligning yourself to God's purpose for you. It moves you farther away. Filling our minds with ungodly things naturally takes us away from dwelling on Godly things. What are you not doing now spiritually that you used to do? Less time in the Word? Less time praying? Thinking more worldly and less spiritually? Little escapes are like putting pavers on a road away from God. (Philippians 4:8)

4. Take control of your first reaction to difficult or undesirable situations.

I have made a commitment to pray more frequently during a difficult situation or when I start to feel anxious. My initial reaction was typically to think the worst about any situation and wallow in self-defeating thoughts. Take control of your thoughts and your mind. (2 Corinthians 10:5; Philippians 4:8)

5. Remember God's purpose for you.

In God's loving sovereignty, He has ordained all the circumstances that you have in your life for your sanctification, to mold you into the image of Christ. (Isaiah 64:8; Romans 8:29; 2 Corinthians 3:18)

6. Trust in God's purposes for you.

When God allowed Babylon to capture Jerusalem and exile the Israelites for 70 years, God told them: "For thus says the Lord: When seventy years are completed for Babylon, I will visit you, and I will fulfill to you my promise and bring you back to this place. For I know the plans I have for you, declares the Lord, plans for welfare and not for evil, to give you a future and a hope" (Jeremiah 29: 10-11). Even in difficult circumstances, God's plans are good for us.

7. Remember God's purpose for work.

In our work, God has graciously invited us to participate in His creation and in a deeper relationship with Him by enjoying our God-given gifts to encourage and build the Body of Christ, to sanctify His people, for His glory (Genesis 2:15).

8. Find accountability.

Confide in a Christian brother or sister about your escapism. I think you will be surprised in the commonalities you share. Meet regularly to discuss each other's progress.

Finally, if you are truly one of God's children, you will never escape from God's loving hand. You will never escape from His purposes and lessons in your life (Psalm 139: 7-12).

God had directed Jonah to call the great city of Nineveh to repentance. Jonah sought to remove himself from this calling by escaping to Tarshish. God's purposes were not thwarted. You know the story of Jonah and the great fish. Jonah called the city of Nineveh to repentance, and they responded by humbly submitting themselves before the Lord. But Jonah was angry that God relented from destroying the city of Nineveh. Jonah then escaped from witnessing God's mercy toward Nineveh to sit under a tree east of the city. He chose not to participate in God's loving grace toward His children.

That is what we are truly missing when we seek to escape. We are missing God's hand at work in the situation and in our lives. We miss out on witnessing His strength, His mercy, His grace, and His incredible power. But God, in His continuing mercy, doesn't want us to miss out and may choose to keep us in the environment to witness Him and learn the lessons He has for us. He loves us that much!

For Further Study

1. What are your first avenues of escape?
2. Imagine that you become financially independent and no longer have to work. Will this truly remove the sin of escapism?
3. Read Luke 12:16-20. Is our spiritual goal to pursue a comfortable life of ease? Where did the rich man's abundance come from? As a result, what was his responsibility?
4. What are some ways to replace the attitude of escapism in your work life?
5. In what ways has escapism impacted your life spiritually?
6. Read Matthew 11:28-30. Instead of escaping, where does Christ tell us to go?

Chapter 24

Losing a Job

I once partnered with a fellow believer in what I thought was an outstanding business venture with tremendous upside potential. The business model included working with and soliciting top-tier professional athletes. It was an exciting opportunity and I had fully convinced myself that this is where the Lord was leading. Why would the Lord present this tremendous opportunity if He didn't want me to succeed? I quit my steady-paying job to pursue this venture in another state. Through a variety of events, the business venture did not take off as we expected. Fortunately, my family and I had not yet moved but we had already sold our house. We were left homeless and without income. We decided to remain in our current city where we had connections, to rent a place to live, and to find a new job.

I was devastated and lost. We had young children at the time, and I was the sole financial provider of my family. I questioned the Lord, but it actually was a poor life decision on my part. I realize now that I was blinded by the potential worldly status and success that this opportunity would bring. I didn't heed or listen to wise counsel that questioned my thought process. I only gave it a passive commitment to prayer because this is what "I wanted to happen." I had followed my ego and pride rather than prudence and learned some valuable life lessons.

Anyone in the working world could potentially find themselves out of a job for one reason or another. This is a pivotal event in our lives. Our response and reaction to this situation can be extremely spiritually sanctifying and lead to a deeper relationship with Christ or tempt us to discouragement and doubt and a turning away from Him.

Perhaps your job loss is a business workforce reduction. Perhaps it is a result of losing the trust of a superior through no fault of your own, or perhaps it is because of a poor personal decision. Regardless, I hazard to guess that most of us have been "between jobs" and without work or income at one time in our lives.

The period between paychecks is extremely difficult emotionally, on you *and* your family. Understanding this impact is fundamental in working together to bridge the gap, both emotionally and financially.

No matter the situation or circumstances, God is sovereign and in control, therefore He has a purpose.

> *"And we know that for those who love God all things work together for good, for those who are called according to his purpose. For those whom he foreknew he also predestined to be conformed to the image of his Son, in order that he might be the firstborn among many brothers. And those whom he predestined he also called, and those whom he called he also justified, and those whom he justified he also glorified." (Romans 8:28-30)*

If we genuinely believe that God is sovereign, which He is, He is sovereign over our circumstances and even over our mistakes.

If you find yourself in this situation where you are out of work, the questions to ask are: How did I truly get here? What is God teaching me through this? How is God glorified in this? Finally, what are my next steps?

There are many steps that you should take to seek the answers to these questions. Let's discuss the thought processes you can take yourself through.

1. How did you get here?

If it was a workforce reduction due to a business decline, first determine if it was an external or internal factor that led to this decline. Obviously, there are many external economic factors outside of our control that may lead to a workforce reduction: company leadership not reacting to business trends, changes in federal/state regulations, advances in technology, etc. Not to discount those, there are just as many internal factors to consider as well. Did you as a business leader participate in any poor business practices or decisions that contributed to this decline, or fail to take corrective action that could have prevented it?

I once heard a wise leader's response during an economic recession several years earlier. He said, "I refuse to participate in it." What he meant was that he would make the necessary and creative business course corrections to keep his company viable during tough economic times. A bridge and road construction company that I worked for was founded in 1918. During WWII, the infrastructure industry declined with all resources being devoted to the war effort. So the family ownership arranged to build magnesium bomb casings for the U.S. military during the war. This was a completely different industry, but this course change provided them with the necessary income to keep their company afloat.

Did you make any bad decisions as an employee that led to the company's decline? If so, make sure you gained some valuable business experience as a result. Determine if your individual performance had any impact on the performance of the company. Have your manager or others been telling you that your performance is not up to their standards, and you refused to listen or take corrective action? Learn from these mistakes. Many times, during the course of a workforce reduction, individual performance is the determining factor in the order of reduction and is an opportunity for a struggling organization to remove excessive overhead or poor performing employees. Don't be the employee that the organization seeks to eliminate in the first wave. Always be the employee that the organization wants to retain in the case of an economic downturn and can help turn things around. Make yourself invaluable in the business recovery. You may need to adjust your career objectives from individual success measurements to organizational survival (which is a good long-term lesson).

Conduct an honest evaluation as to the root cause of your job elimination and learn from it. Don't automatically lay blame on external factors; look deeply as to what internal factors you could have addressed that may have prevented, or at least postponed, your workforce reduction. More than likely, there will be an internal answer to that question and personal actions that you can take or could have taken. Look internally first. Humbly seek feedback from those who are releasing you. Some people may be honest with you, but others may not for fear of legal repercussions. Ask anyway.

2. Did this job loss come because of a personal injury or medical issue?

These are difficult situations to submit to, especially if you have relied on your expertise in your field all your working life.

There are obviously programs and medical plans that you can take advantage of in these situations, but most of them are short-term solutions. If your current employer cannot accommodate your new physical restrictions, you may need to adjust your career to your new physical limitations (e.g., becoming a consultant or learning a new skill).

3. If you were terminated, what was the determining factor?

A lot of times, these are totally within our control. It could have been a failure to perform to the expectations of the job, or worse, a character issue. Be honest with yourself. Was this termination because of something you did or did not do? Correct this immediately to avoid having the same result at your next job. I have seen many terminated employees blame their employer or boss for their failure to succeed in the role and they do this at the next job and the next and the one after that. It becomes a pattern with them. Humbly seek your heart and determine if you see this pattern in your own life. Confess your personal mistakes and sin in the loss of your job. Take personal ownership and responsibility to avoid this in the future.

4. Were you treated unfairly?

There are other times when a manager is unjustifiably seeking to force a good performing individual out of the organization. If this is the case, you are better off. Perhaps this is God's way of removing you from an unpleasant work situation and leading you elsewhere. Admittedly, that does not make the impact of the termination any easier or ease the loss of income. But, if you have done everything that God has asked you to do in this situation, then the main thing you can do is to trust Him through it.

5. What is God teaching you through this? How is He glorified?

Remember, God's purpose is to conform us to the image of Christ, not to guarantee material success. A job loss resulting in a loss of income, regardless of the reason, is a tremendously sanctifying experience. Don't squander the opportunity. Use this time to grow closer to Christ and His desire for you to trust Him. His desire and will for all His children are for us to know and trust Him more today than yesterday. God desires a deeper relationship with us, and He uses every situation to teach us how to do this, even a job loss.

6. What are next steps?

Don't let the experience overwhelm you to the point of inaction. Obtaining new employment is now your new full-time job. However, don't be discouraged or impatient if God does not immediately provide new employment. Pray daily for renewed strength to carry you through this time: *"But they who wait for the Lord shall renew their strength; they shall mount up with wings like eagles; they shall run and not be weary; they shall walk and not faint"* (Isaiah 40:31). Update your resume, connect with current or former co-workers for potential employment, or if your industry is declining, update your skill set with training and education. Find job boards in your industry and post your resume on every job site that you can. There is also nothing wrong with finding temporary employment to make ends meet financially. Don't wait for internal motivation; action leads to motivation.

You may believe or feel like God is punishing you. God is not a God of continual punishment. He does not delight in that. You did not lose your job because God hates you. You are not suffering because God hates you. (Consider Job's afflictions.) Conversely, while He does allow the freedom for us to make certain decisions, we suffer the consequences of bad decisions. Some of us only learn by consistently attending the "School of Hard Knocks," if you will. Even in this, God is with us, and He delights when we turn to Him as a loving Father and rest in His loving care.

Continue to seek God's wisdom through this time. Have you turned away from God to pursue your own way and thus are suffering the consequences of that decision? Or is God preparing you for a new career or encouraging you in a direction for His purposes, which you may not see yet? Whatever the circumstances, through His sovereign will, God is providing you with an opportunity to lean on Him through submission and obedience to Him. Trust His love and will for you, even after losing a job.

For Further Study

1. Read Psalm 22. How does this relate to the losing a job or being out of work?
2. Read 1 Corinthians 10:31. What does excellent work look like? Can always doing excellent work guarantee continued employment? Why or why not? If not, then what is the purpose of doing your work to the glory of God?
3. Read Romans 8:15-16. Why is this important to remember during this period of transition?
4. Read Proverbs 12:1. How would this apply to an individual losing a job? Why?

Final Thoughts

I hope and pray that the subjects addressed here have been encouraging and helpful to you. I certainly realize that your situation or circumstance may not have been specifically addressed in these chapters. I can understand the reactions of, "Yeah, but you don't know my boss/employees/co-workers/organization. They're different." That is absolutely true.

One thing I have learned in my career is that every workplace issue has differing dynamics, personalities, and circumstances. No two issues are the same. If they were, then a simple and straightforward policy manual would be universally adopted. Every issue would have a prescribed procedure and outcome.

However, if your company is anything like the ones I have worked in, company policies and procedures are constantly being revised and updated. We cannot rely on corporate policies to remain consistent for any length of time. But God is reliable and consistent. His Word is proven and true. Scripture is "breathed out by God and profitable for teaching, for reproof, for correction, and for training in righteousness, that the man (or woman) of God may be complete, equipped for every good work" (2 Timothy 3:16-17).

The inerrant Word of God is "living and active, sharper than any two-edged sword, piercing to the division of soul and of spirit, of joints and of marrow, and discerning the thoughts and intentions of the heart" (Hebrews 4:12). God and His Word are the only consistent and dependable aspects of the Christian walk. Even our own spiritual walk is subject to change due to our human failures and ever-changing growth.

Why would we not rely and depend on the inerrancy and reliability of Scripture to guide us through all of life's circumstances . . . even those at work?

If you have a specific workplace issue or situation
that you would like to discuss,
please contact me directly:
http://biblicalhr.com/free-consultation

In Him alone,
Brett

About the Author

Brett Billups has been a follower of Christ for over 25 years and has been an HR professional for almost as long. Brett has served in both the private and public sectors in various positions including leading the HR function for one of the nation's largest employee-owned organizations. His broad career experience has provided him with a unique business perspective from field operations to the Boardroom. His pursuit of Christian development in the workplace led him to found Biblical HR, LLC in 2021 based in the Dallas-Fort Worth Metroplex. Brett and his wife Krissi have four grown children and a growing number of special grandchildren. They reside in Flower Mound, TX.

A free ebook edition
is available with the
purchase of this book.

To claim your free ebook edition:

1. Visit MorganJamesBOGO.com
2. Sign your name CLEARLY in the space
3. Complete the form and submit a photo of
   the entire copyright page
4. You or your friend can download the ebook
   to your preferred device

Print & Digital Together Forever.

Snap a photo   Free ebook   Read anywhere

CPSIA information can be obtained
at www.ICGtesting.com
Printed in the USA
JSHW020224190422
25075JS00001B/29

9 781631 956829